HBR Guide to
Delivering
Effective
Feedback

Harvard Business Review Guides

Arm yourself with the advice you need to succeed on the job, from the most trusted brand in business. Packed with how-to essentials from leading experts, the HBR Guides provide smart answers to your most pressing work challenges.

The titles include:

HBR Guide to Better Business Writing

HBR Guide to Building Your Business Case

HBR Guide to Buying a Small Business

HBR Guide to Coaching Employees

HBR Guide to Delivering Effective Feedback

HBR Guide to Finance Basics for Managers

HBR Guide to Getting the Mentoring You Need

HBR Guide to Getting the Right Job

HBR Guide to Getting the Right Work Done

HBR Guide to Leading Teams

HBR Guide to Making Every Meeting Matter

HBR Guide to Managing Conflict at Work

HBR Guide to Managing Stress at Work

HBR Guide to Managing Up and Across

HBR Guide to Negotiating

HBR Guide to Networking

HBR Guide to Office Politics

HBR Guide to Persuasive Presentations

HBR Guide to Project Management

HBR Guide to
Delivering
Effective
Feedback

HARVARD BUSINESS REVIEW PRESS

Boston, Massachusetts

Quantity Sales Discounts

HBR Business Review Press titles are available at significant discounts when purchased in bulk for client gifts, sales quantities, and premiums. Special editions, including books with corporate logos, customized covers, and letters from the company CEO printed the front matter, as well as excerpts of existing books, can be created in large quantities for special needs.

For details and discount information for both print and ebook formats, contact booksales@harvardbusiness.org, tel. 800-988-0886, or www.hbr.org/bulksales.

Copyright 2016 Harvard Business School Publishing Corporation

The web addresses referenced in this book were live and correct at the time of the book's publication but may be subject to change.

Library of Congress Cataloging-in-Publication Data

Names: Harvard Business Review Press, issuing body.
Title: HBR guide to delivering effective feedback / Harvard Business
    Review Press.
Description: Boston, Massachusetts : Harvard Business Review Press,
    [2016]
Identifiers: LCCN 2015047167 | ISBN 9781633695528

Subjects: LCSH: Employee retention. | Feedback (Psychology) |
    Employees—Rating of. | Personnel management.
Classification: LCC HF5549.5.R58 H424 2016 | DDC 658.3/14—dc23
    LC record available at http://lccn.loc.gov/2015047167

What You'll Learn

Are you worried about losing your star performer to greener pastures? Or struggling with a problem employee? Do you dread annual performance appraisals?

As a manager, you know it's important to give your employees the feedback they need to develop. But communicating it in a way that motivates them to improve can be a challenge. And the prospect of facing someone who may get emotional can seem overwhelming.

But whether you are discussing a formal performance assessment or addressing everyday behavior, you can transform these stressful encounters into productive conversations. Brimming with actionable advice on everything from delivering constructive comments to recognizing exceptional work, this guide will give you the tools and confidence you need to master giving effective feedback to your direct reports.

You'll learn how to:

- Incorporate ongoing feedback into your daily interactions with employees

- Transform annual appraisals into catalysts for growth

- Plan for a tense conversation with a combative recipient

- Provide a clear message that emphasizes improvement

- Identify the reasons behind performance issues—including your own role

- Motivate individuals by acknowledging accomplishments

- Coach your star to the next level

- Measure performance when results aren't easily quantified

- Establish goals that will help your people develop

- Communicate criticism effectively across global cultures

- Engage your team during feedback discussions

Contents

Section 2: FORMAL PERFORMANCE APPRAISALS

Section 3: TOUGH TOPICS

Contents

Section 1
Ongoing Feedback

Chapter 1
Giving Effective Feedback

If you're like most managers, the prospect of giving feedback to your employees can be nerve-racking. Perhaps you're worried about how your staff will react. Or maybe you're doubtful that your comments will make a difference in their work or behavior.

But feedback is a vital tool for ensuring that your employees are developing in your organization. A feedback discussion is an opportunity for you to share your observations with your employees about their job performance and elicit productive change. Without it, they will have no idea of how you see them. Avoid having a tough conversation with your underperformers early on, and their performance (and possibly your team's) plummets.

Adapted from *Giving Feedback* (product #348X), *Performance Appraisal* (product #12352), both from the Pocket Mentor series, and the 20-Minute Manager series books *Giving Effective Feedback* (product #13999) and *Performance Reviews* (product #15035)

Assume that your high performers know their value and will keep up the good work, and they may start "phoning it in" or leave your company altogether to advance their careers.

Feedback increases employees' self-awareness and fosters positive change throughout the organization. There are two main types: **Ongoing feedback** occurs on a regular or ad hoc basis; it can be delivered up (to your boss), down (to your employees), or across the organizational chart (to your peers). **Formal feedback**, typically shared during annual or semiannual performance reviews, tends to be between you and your direct report. This guide will prepare you to discuss both types with your employees.

Ongoing Feedback

Grounded in the goals you and your employees have set together at the beginning of the year, ongoing feedback provides opportunities for early intervention if someone is not hitting the mark. It also allows you to recognize and reinforce good work. Ongoing feedback includes on-the-spot conversations (for example, constructive comments about an employee's presentation delivery at a board meeting), the weekly check-in meetings you have with each member of your team to gauge progress on both little- and big-picture objectives, and career coaching sessions. Such frequent interactions not only help keep people on track but also make it easier for you to prepare your formal annual appraisal. By taking note of your observations and discussing your employees' progress throughout the year, you'll already know where your direct reports' strengths and weaknesses lie, and your employees will already be working on areas for improvement and development before the formal feedback session.

Formal Feedback

Formal feedback enables you to summarize all the evaluations and support you've provided throughout the year. Like ongoing feedback, these yearly assessments afford you the opportunity to identify what's going well with an employee's performance and to diagnose problems before they worsen. This discussion shouldn't contain any surprises: You'll have already talked about performance issues in your ongoing feedback sessions, as well as expectations that affect pay, merit increases, bonuses, and promotions. But the formal review also gives you the chance to plan for the future. It allows you and your direct reports to discuss where they might develop and collaborate on new goals for the upcoming year, so they can move forward in their job and career.

Think of both ongoing and formal feedback as part of a partnership with your employees, one that promotes trust and candid dialogue. For example, encourage them to pinpoint factors that support or impede their work; they can do this in the face-to-face discussion or in a written self-assessment in advance of the meeting. Perhaps solidifying relationships with team members through lunches or after-work drinks is helping them achieve important objectives. Or maybe difficulty controlling e-mail tone is alienating key IT project managers. Encourage them to also note achievements ("I closed two new deals worth $100,000 and established a weekly check-in with our new distributor") and identify resources they need for future development (such as training on a new sales-reporting system or a mentor to advise them in a new job function).

Given how widespread the fear of feedback is (on both sides of the exchange), you may think you can't possibly overcome your anxiety and have a meaningful conversation with your direct report. But you can—and the articles in this guide will help.

Chapter 2
Sometimes Negative Feedback Is Best

by Heidi Grant Halvorson

If I see one more article about how you should never be "critical" or "negative" when giving feedback to an employee or colleague, I think my head will explode. It's incredibly frustrating. This kind of advice is undoubtedly well meant, and it certainly *sounds* good. After all, you probably don't relish the thought of having to tell someone else what they are doing wrong—at minimum, it's a little embarrassing for both of you.

But avoiding negative feedback is both wrongheaded and dangerous. *Wrongheaded* because, when delivered the right way, at the right time, criticism is in fact highly motivating. *Dangerous* because without awareness of the

---

Adapted from content posted on hbr.org on January 28, 2013

mistakes they are making, no one can possibly improve. Staying "positive" when doling out feedback will only get you so far.

Hang on, you say. *Can't negative feedback be discouraging? Demotivating?*

That's perfectly true.

And don't people need encouragement to feel confident? Doesn't that help them stay motivated?

In many cases, yes.

Confusing, isn't it? Thankfully, brilliant research by Stacey Finkelstein from Columbia University and Ayelet Fishbach from the University of Chicago sheds light on the seemingly paradoxical nature of feedback by making it clear why, when, and for whom negative feedback is appropriate.

It's important to begin by understanding the function that positive and negative feedback serve. Praise (for instance, *Here's what you did really well . . .*) increases *commitment* to the work you do by enhancing both your experience and your confidence. A more critical assessment (for example, *Here's where you went wrong . . .*), on the other hand, is *informative*—it tells you where you need to spend your effort and offers insight into how you might improve.

Given these two different functions, positive and negative feedback should be more effective (and more motivating) for different people at different times. For instance, when you don't really know what you are doing, encouragement helps you to stay optimistic and feel more at ease with the challenges you are facing—something *novices* tend to need. But when you are an *expert* and you already more or less know what you are doing, it's constructive criticism that can help you do what it takes to get to the top of your game.

As Finkelstein and Fishbach show, novices and experts are indeed looking for, and motivated by, different kinds of information. In one of their studies, American students taking either beginner or advanced-level French classes were asked whether they would prefer an instructor who emphasized what they were doing right (focusing on their strengths) or what they were doing wrong (focusing on their mistakes and how to correct them). Beginners overwhelmingly preferred a cheerleading, strength-focused instructor. Advanced students, on the other hand, preferred a more critical instructor who would help them develop their weaker skills.

In a second study, the researchers looked at a very different behavior: engaging in environmentally friendly actions. Their "experts" were members of environmental organizations (for instance, Greenpeace), while their "novices" were nonmembers. Each participant in the study made a list of the actions they regularly took that helped the environment—things like recycling, avoiding bottled water, and taking shorter showers. They were offered feedback from an environmental consultant on the effectiveness of their actions, and were given a choice: Would you prefer to know more about the actions you take that *are* effective, or about the actions you take that are *not*? Experts were much more likely to choose the negative feedback—about ineffective actions—than novices.

Taken together, these studies show that people who are experienced in a given domain—people who already have developed some knowledge and skills—don't actually live in fear of negative feedback. If anything, they seek it out. Intuitively they realize that negative feedback offers the key to getting ahead, while positive feedback merely tells them what they already know.

But what about motivation? What kind of feedback makes you want to take action? When participants in the environmental study were *randomly* given either positive or negative feedback about their actions, and were then asked how much of their $25 study compensation they would like to donate to Greenpeace, the type of feedback they received had a dramatic effect on their motivation to give. When negative feedback was given, experts gave more on average to Greenpeace ($8.53) than novices ($1.24). But when positive feedback was given, novices ($8.31) gave far more than experts ($2.92).

I'm not suggesting that you never tell rookies about their mistakes, or that you never praise seasoned professionals for their outstanding work. And of course, negative feedback should always be accompanied by good advice and given with tact.

But I *am* suggesting that piling on praise is a more effective motivator for the rookie than the pro. And I'm saying, point blank, that you shouldn't worry so much when it comes to identifying mistakes with someone experienced. Negative feedback won't crush their confidence—it just might give them the information they need to take their performance to the next level.

Heidi Grant Halvorson, PhD, is associate director for the Motivation Science Center at the Columbia University Business School and author of *Nine Things Successful People Do Differently* and *No One Understands You and What to Do about It.*

Chapter 3
Giving Feedback That Sticks

by Ed Batista

"Can I give you some feedback?"

When you ask your employees this question, their heart rate and blood pressure are almost certain to increase, and they may experience other signs of stress as well. These are symptoms of a "threat response," also known as "fight-or-flight": a cascade of neurological and physiological events that impair the ability to process complex information and react thoughtfully. When people are in the grip of a threat response, they're less capable of absorbing and applying your observations.

You've probably noticed this dynamic in feedback conversations that didn't go as well as you'd hoped. Some

---

Adapted from the *HBR Guide to Coaching Employees* (product #13990), Harvard Business Review Press, 2015 people respond with explanations, defensiveness, or even hostility, while others minimize eye contact, cross their arms, hunch over, and generally look as if they'd rather be doing anything but talking to you. These fight-or-flight behaviors suggest that your comments probably won't have their desired impact.

How do you avoid triggering a threat response—and deliver feedback your people can digest and use? The guidelines that follow will help.

Cultivate the Relationship

We lay the foundations for effective feedback by building relationships with others over time. When people feel connected to us, even difficult conversations with them are less likely to trigger a threat response. Social psychologist John Gottman, a leading expert on building relationships, has found from his research that success in difficult conversations depends on what he calls "the quality of the friendship." Gottman cites several steps we can take to develop high-quality relationships:

- **Make the other person feel "known."** Making people aware that you see them as individuals—and not merely as employees—is a critical step in the process, but it need not be overly time-consuming. Several years ago, a coaching client of mine who ran a midsize company felt that he was too distant from his employees but didn't have the time to take someone to lunch every day. His efficient compromise was to view every interaction, no matter how fleeting, as an opportunity to get to know that person a little better. He made a habit of asking employees one question about their work or their personal lives each time he encountered them. "Whenever I can, I connect," he told me. Although at times this slowed his progress through the office, the result was worth it.

- **Respond to even small bids for attention.** We seek attention from those around us not only in obvious ways but also through countless subtle "bids." As Gottman writes in *The Relationship Cure,* "A bid can be a question, a gesture, a look, a touch—any single expression that says, 'I want to feel connected to you.' A response to a bid is just that—a positive or negative answer to somebody's request for emotional connection." But many of us miss bids from our employees. That's because we're less observant of social cues from people over whom we wield authority, according to research by Dacher Keltner of the University of California, Berkeley, and others. To connect more effectively with employees, take stock of how much you notice—or have missed previously—their efforts to gain your attention. And solicit feedback from peers, friends, and family members on your listening skills and how often you interrupt.

- **Regularly express appreciation.** As Gottman's research shows, the ratio of positive to negative interactions in a successful relationship is 5:1, even during periods of conflict. This ratio doesn't apply to a single conversation, and it doesn't mean that we're obligated to pay someone five compliments before we can offer critical feedback (in fact, doing so could confuse your message). But it does highlight the importance of providing positive feedback and expressing other forms of appreciation over time in order to strengthen the relationship. (See the sidebar "The Pitfalls of Positive Feedback.")

THE PITFALLS OF POSITIVE FEEDBACK

Praise is supposed to make your employees feel good and motivate them, but often it does just the opposite. Here are three common problems and ways to avoid them:

1. ***People don't trust the praise.*** Before delivering unpleasant feedback to your direct reports, do you say something nice to soften the blow? Many of us do—and thus unwittingly condition people to hear our positive feedback as a hollow preamble to the real message. Rather than feeling genuinely appreciated, they're waiting for the other shoe to drop. Though you've diminished your anxiety about bearing bad news, you haven't helped your direct reports receive it. You've actually undermined your ability to deliver any meaningful feedback, positive or negative.

   What to do: Instead of giving a spoonful of sugar before every dose of constructive criticism, lead off with your investment in the relationship and your reasons for having the conversation. For example: "It's important that we can be candid and direct with each other so we can work together effectively. I have some concerns for us to discuss, and I'm optimistic that we can resolve them."

2. **People resent it.** Managers also use positive feedback to overcome resistance to requests. This age-old tactic can work in the moment but carries a long-term cost. It creates a sense of obligation, a "social debt" the recipient feels compelled to repay by acceding to your wishes. But if you train people to always expect requests after your praise, they'll eventually feel manipulated and resentful—and less inclined to help you out.

   What to do: Motivate people over the long term by expanding your persuasive tool kit. As Jay Conger explains in his classic article "The Necessary Art of Persuasion" (HBR May–June 1998), you can gain lasting influence in four ways: establish credibility through expertise and work you've done in others' interests, frame goals around common ground and shared advantage, support your views with compelling data and examples, and connect emotionally with people so they'll be more receptive to your message.

   (continued)

THE PITFALLS OF POSITIVE FEEDBACK

(*continued*)

3. *We praise the wrong things.* When aimed at the wrong targets, praise does more harm than good. As Stanford psychologist Carol Dweck notes in a January 2012 HBR IdeaCast interview, "The whole self-esteem movement taught us erroneously that praising intelligence, talent, and abilities would foster self-confidence and self-esteem, and everything great would follow. But we've found it backfires. People who are praised for talent now worry about doing the next thing, about taking on the hard task, and not looking talented, tarnishing that reputation for brilliance. So they'll stick to their comfort zones and get really defensive when they hit setbacks."

What to do: Praise effort, not ability. Dweck suggests focusing on "the strategies, the doggedness and persistence, the grit and resilience" that people exhibit when facing challenges. And explain exactly what actions prompted your praise. If you're vague or generic, you'll fail to reinforce the desired behavior.

Set the Stage

Once you've laid the groundwork with your employee, prepare for a feedback discussion by considering logistics. It's easy to take our surroundings for granted, but they have a big impact on any interaction. Paying attention to details like these will help make your conversations more productive:

- **Timing.** Be deliberate about scheduling a feedback session, whether it is a shorter, informal conversation or a longer, in-depth discussion. Instead of simply fitting it into an available slot on your calendar, choose a time when you and the other person will both be at your best, such as at the beginning of the day, before you're preoccupied with other issues, or at the end of the day, when you can spend more time in reflection. Think about the activities you and your employee will be engaged in just before and just after you meet. If either of you are coming from (or heading to) a stressful experience, you'll be better off finding another time.

- **Duration.** We often put events on our calendars for a standard amount of time without considering what's really needed for each interaction. Think about how much time a given feedback conversation is likely to take if it goes well—and if it goes poorly. You don't want to get into a meaningful discussion with an employee and suddenly find that you're late for your next meeting. Also, consider what you'll do if the session goes worse (or better) than expected. How bad (or good) will it have to be for you to ignore the next event on your calendar in order to continue the conversation?

- **Physical location.** Meeting in your office will reinforce hierarchical roles, which can be useful when you need to establish some distance between yourself and the other person—but this will also induce stress and increase the odds of a threat response. A less formal setting—such as a conference room, a restaurant, or even outdoors—will put you on a more even footing and reduce the likelihood of a threat response. Choose a location that suits the needs of the conversation, ensures sufficient privacy, and minimizes interruptions and distractions.

- **Proximity.** When meeting with an employee in an office or a conference room, sitting across from each other over a desk or table creates physical distance, emphasizing your respective roles and reinforcing your authority. But you don't always want to do that. When you're trying to create a stronger connection with the other person or convey a greater sense of empathy, it's preferable to sit closer and on adjoining sides of the table or desk. Think about the optimal proximity between you and the other person at that moment. Perhaps even being seated is too formal, and you should go for a walk.

Focus on Facts, Not Assumptions

Next, concentrate on the message you want to convey. You're sure to elicit a threat response if you provide feedback the other person views as unfair or inaccurate. Your feedback should address their performance based on the goals and targets you set at the beginning of the year. But sometimes this assessment isn't black and white. How do you avoid a negative reaction, given how subjective perceptions of fairness and accuracy are?

David Bradford of the Stanford Graduate School of Business suggests "staying on our side of the net"—that is, focusing our feedback on our feelings about the behavior and avoiding references to the other person's motives. We're in safe territory on our side of the net; others may not like what we say when we describe how we feel, but they can't dispute its accuracy. However, when we make guesses about their motives, we cross over to their side of the net, and even minor inaccuracies can provoke a defensive reaction.

For example, when giving critical feedback to someone who's habitually late, it's tempting to say something like, "You don't value my time, and it's very disrespectful of you." But these are guesses about the other person's state of mind, not statements of fact. If we're even slightly off base, the employee will feel misunderstood and be less receptive to the feedback. A more effective way to make the same point is to say, "When you're late, I feel devalued and disrespected." It's a subtle distinction, but by focusing on the specific behavior and our internal response, we avoid making an inaccurate, disputable guess.

Because motives are often unclear, we constantly cross the net in an effort to make sense of others' behavior. While this is inevitable, it's good practice to notice when we're guessing someone's motives and get back on our side of the net before offering feedback. (For more on framing the feedback discussion, see the next chapter, "A Better Way to Deliver Bad News.")

Manage Emotions

Although excessive negative feelings inhibit learning and communication, emotions play a vital role in feedback. They convey emphasis and let others know what we value. Emotional experiences stick with people, last longer in their memories, and are easier to recall. And extensive neuroscience research in recent decades makes clear that emotions are essential to our reasoning process: Strong emotions can pull us off course, but in general emotions support better decision making.

So while you'll want to avoid triggering a threat response, don't remove all emotion from your discussion. That can diminish the impact of your feedback and lead to a cycle of ineffective conversations. Instead, aim for a balance: Express *just enough* emotion to engage the other person but not so much that you provoke a hostile or defensive reaction, shut down the conversation, or damage the relationship. (If you do anticipate a combative response, see chapter 15, "Delivering Criticism to a Defensive Employee.")

The right amount of emotion depends on the issue you're addressing and varies from one relationship to another—and even from one day to the next. The key question is how responsive the other person will be to your emotions. A coaching client of mine who'd recently launched a company had some critical feedback for his cofounder, but previous conversations didn't have the desired effect. For the feedback to stick, my client needed to become fairly heated and more vocally and physically expressive. This worked because the two of them had a long-standing friendship. The cofounder didn't respond defensively—rather, the intensity got his attention. In contrast, when this same client had some critical feedback for a subordinate, he reined in his emotions, modulated his expressiveness, and delivered the feedback in a matter-of-fact tone. The goal was to convey the importance of the issues without overwhelming the subordinate, and in this case, my client's authority was sufficient on its own.

Of course, we may not know how another person will respond to our emotions, and when we're in the grip of strong feelings, it's hard to calibrate how we express them in conversation. The solution is to practice. By having more feedback conversations, we learn not only how specific individuals respond to us but also how we express our emotions in helpful and unhelpful ways.

Rehearse and Repeat

With a little practice, these guidelines will help you improve your feedback skills. As with any skill you're trying to master, experiment in low-risk situations before jumping into a high-stakes feedback conversation. Here are a few ways to make feedback a habit and improve your skills:

- **Have feedback conversations more often.** Rather than saving up feedback for an employee on a wide range of topics during a performance review, offer smaller pieces of focused feedback on a regular basis. Even a two-minute debrief with an employee after a meeting or a presentation can be a useful learning opportunity for both of you. The sidebar, "When to Give Feedback," provides some recommendations for when feedback would be beneficial, as well as when it wouldn't.

- **Role-play difficult conversations.** With clients in my coaching practice and with my MBA students at Stanford, I've found that role-playing is a highly effective way to prepare to deliver challenging feedback. Conduct this exercise with a friendly colleague: Start by delivering your feedback while your colleague role-plays the recipient, which will allow you to try out different approaches. Then have your colleague give you the same feedback while you role-play the recipient. You'll learn from your colleague's approach, and you'll see the conversation from your employee's point of view. The preparation will help you refine your delivery and feel more relaxed in the actual conversation.

- **Ask for feedback yourself.** By asking employees to give you feedback on your effectiveness as a leader and manager, you'll benefit in three ways: You'll get valuable input; you'll understand what it's like to be on the receiving end; and your willingness to listen will make your own feedback mean more. If you sense that employees are reluctant to give you feedback, ask them to help you accomplish some specific goals, such as being more concise or interrupting less often. By acknowledging your own areas for improvement, you'll make it easier for them to speak up.

WHEN TO GIVE FEEDBACK

As you practice giving feedback more often, you'll learn when a behavior warrants immediate feedback. Until then, here are some suggestions as to when it is an opportune time to meet with your employee—and when you should avoid it.

Offering feedback can be most useful in the following instances:

- When good work, successful projects, and resourceful behavior deserve to be recognized

- When the likelihood of improving a person's skills is high, because the opportunity to use those skills again is imminent

- When the person is already expecting feedback, either because a feedback session was scheduled in advance or because she knows that you observed the behavior

- When a problem cannot be ignored, because the person's behavior is negatively affecting a colleague, the team, or the organization

In other cases, feedback can be detrimental to the situation. Avoid giving feedback in these circumstances:

- When you do not have all the information about a given incident

(continued)

WHEN TO GIVE FEEDBACK

(*continued*)

- When the only feedback you can offer concerns factors that the recipient cannot easily change or control

- When the person who needs the feedback appears to be highly emotional or especially vulnerable immediately after a difficult event

- When you do not have the time or the patience to deliver the feedback in a calm and thorough manner

- When the feedback is based on your personal preference, not a need for more effective behavior

- When you have not yet formulated a possible solution to help the feedback recipient move forward

Bear in mind that when you give positive feedback frequently, your negative feedback, when it is warranted, will seem more credible and less threatening. Offering input only when problems arise may cause people to see you as unappreciative or petty.

Adapted from *Giving Effective Feedback* (20-Minute Manager series) (product #13999), Harvard Business Review Press, 2014.

Ed Batista is an executive coach and an instructor at the Stanford Graduate School of Business. He writes regularly on issues related to coaching and professional development at www.edbatista.com, and he is currently writing a book on self-coaching for Harvard Business Review Press.

Chapter 4
A Better Way to Deliver Bad News

by Jean-François Manzoni

A summary of the full-length HBR article by Jean-François Manzoni, highlighting key ideas.

IDEA IN BRIEF

That dreaded moment has come: You're delivering critical feedback to an employee. Despite your best efforts, the conversation is a disaster: tempers flare, the employee gets defensive, your relationship grows strained.

What happened? Like most managers, you probably inadvertently sabotaged the meeting—preparing for it in

Reprinted from *Harvard Business Review*, September 2002 (product #R0209J)

a way that stifled honest discussion and prevented you from delivering feedback effectively.

In other words, you most likely engaged in restrictive framing—a *narrow, binary,* and *frozen* approach to feedback: You initiated the conversation without considering alternative explanations for the problem behavior, assumed a win-or-lose outcome, and rigidly maintained your assumptions during the conversation.

Delivering corrective feedback doesn't have to be so difficult—if you use a more open-minded, flexible approach that convinces employees the process is fair.

IDEA IN PRACTICE

Restrictive Framing

When preparing to give feedback, you may picture relevant events, decide which information to discuss, and define a solution—all *before* the conversation. This framing sets the stage for trouble.

> *Example:* Liam, a VP, hears complaints that Jeremy, a product manager, isn't delegating enough. Liam's framing—"Jeremy's too controlling"—is *narrow* (Liam excludes other possibilities; e.g., Jeremy wants to delegate but doesn't know how) and *binary* (he assumes Jeremy must delegate or his subordinates will leave and he'll burn out). During the conversation, Liam's framing is *frozen* (he neither hears nor addresses Jeremy's objections). Result? Neither Liam nor Jeremy learn from the meeting.

Two Biases

Why do we frame feedback narrowly—despite predictably poor results? Two biases color the feedback process. And the more stressed we are, the more powerful these biases become:

- **Fundamental attribution error.** We often attribute problems to subordinates' disposition ("Jeremy's too controlling") rather than their circumstances (e.g., perhaps Jeremy *is* delegating, but his subordinates have some other ax to grind). Too busy to identify all potential causes and solutions to a problem, we grab the first acceptable one.

- **False consensus effect.** We assume others see situations as we do, and fail to revise our framing during feedback sessions.

Reframing Feedback

To avoid the restrictive-feedback trap, watch for these biases. Consider alternative explanations for problems rather than leaping to conclusions.

Example: Liam frames his concerns about Jeremy openly: "I've heard complaints that Jeremy isn't delegating—and some of his employees are feeling sufficiently frustrated that I'm afraid we'll start losing them. I'd like to find out if Jeremy knows about the complaints, and get his take."

This framing isn't *narrow* (Liam hasn't leapt to conclusions about the problem's causes) or *binary* (it avoids a win-or-lose outcome). And since Liam avoids a preconceived outcome, he has nothing on which to *freeze*. He initiates the conversation openly: "I don't know if you're aware of this—or if it's true—but I've heard that Frank and Joan are anxious to take on more responsibility. What do you think?"

Why Open Framing Works

Open framing shows you have good intentions, the feedback *development* process was fair (you collected all relevant information), and the *communication* process was fair (you listen to and respect employees).

When employees feel they're getting fair feedback, they accept it more willingly—and work to improve performance.

Giving feedback to your employees, particularly when their performances fall short of expectations, is one of the most critical roles you play as a manager. For most people, it's also one of the most dreaded. Such conversations can be very unpleasant—emotions can run high, tempers can flare. And so, fearing that an employee will become defensive and that the conversation will only strain the relationship, the boss all too often inadvertently sabotages the meeting by preparing for it in a way that stifles honest discussion. This is an unintentional—indeed, unconscious—habit that's a byproduct of stress and that makes it difficult to deliver corrective feedback effectively.

The good news is that these conversations don't have to be so hard. By changing the mind-set with which you develop and deliver negative feedback, you can greatly increase the odds that the process will be a success—that you will have productive conversations, that you won't damage relationships, and that your employees will make real improvements in performance. In the pages that follow, I'll describe what goes wrong during these meetings and why. I'll look in detail at how real-life conversations have unfolded and what the managers could have done differently to reach more satisfying outcomes. As a first step, let's look at the way bosses prepare feedback—that is, the way they frame issues in their own minds in advance of a discussion.

Framing Feedback

In an ideal world, a subordinate would accept corrective feedback with an open mind. He or she would ask a few clarifying questions, promise to work on the issues discussed, and show signs of improvement over time. But things don't always turn out this way.

Let's consider the following example. Liam, a vice president at a consumer products company, had heard some complaints about a product manager, Jeremy. (Names and other identifying information for the subjects mentioned in this article have been altered.) Jeremy consistently delivered high-quality work on time, but several of his subordinates had grumbled about his apparent unwillingness to delegate. They felt their contributions weren't valued and that they didn't have an opportunity to learn and grow. What's more, Liam worried that Jeremy's own career prospects would be limited if his focus on the day-to-day details of his subordinates' work kept him from taking on more strategic projects. As his boss,

Liam felt a responsibility to let Jeremy know about his concerns. Here's how the conversation unfolded:

Liam: "I'd like to discuss your work with you. You're doing a great job, and we really value your contributions. But I think you do too much. You have some great people working for you; why not delegate a little more?"

Jeremy: "I don't understand. I delegate when I think it's appropriate. But a lot of people in this company rely on quality work coming out of my department, so I need to stay involved."

Liam: "Yes, and we all appreciate your attention to detail. But your job as a manager is to help your employees grow into new roles and take on more responsibility. Meanwhile, you're so focused on the details that you don't have time to think about the bigger picture, about the direction you're taking this product."

Jeremy: "That's not true. I'm always thinking about the future."

Liam: "I'm just saying, you'd have more time for strategic thinking if you weren't so mired in the day-to-day stuff."

Jeremy: "Are you saying I'm not a strategic thinker?"

Liam: "You're so busy dotting every *i* and crossing every *t* that I just don't know what kind of thinking you're capable of!"

This type of exchange is surprisingly common. Each side pushes his point of view more and more aggressively, and the conversation escalates until a relatively minor difference becomes much more dramatic. (For a visual representation of a deteriorating discussion, see the sidebar "Scripted Escalation.") Often, as Liam did in the preceding conversation, one person or the other unintentionally says something overly critical. Of course, it may not get to that point—one or both parties may choose to give in rather than fight. But either way, escalate or fold, the subordinate probably hasn't accepted the news the boss set out to deliver. Managers tend to attribute such nonacceptance to employees' pride or defensiveness. Indeed, it's not unusual for people to feel defensive about their work or, for that matter, to hold inflated views of their performance and capabilities. But more often than not, the boss is also to blame. Let's examine why.

Whenever we face a decision or situation, we frame it, consciously or not. At its simplest, a frame is the decision maker's image of a situation—that is, the way he or she pictures the circumstances and elements surrounding the decision. The frame defines the boundaries and dimensions of the decision or situation—for instance, which issues will be looked at, which components are in and which are out, how various bits of information will be weighed, how the problem might be solved or a successful outcome determined, and so on. Managers tend to frame difficult situations and decisions in a way that is *narrow* (alternatives aren't included or even considered) and *binary* (there are only two possible outcomes—win or lose). Then, during the feedback discussion, their framing remains *frozen*—unchanged, regardless of the direction the conversation takes.

In anticipation of the conversation with Jeremy, for example, Liam framed the problem in his mind as "Jeremy's too controlling." This is a narrow framing because it excludes many alternative explanations—for instance, "Jeremy would really like to hand off some responsibility but doesn't know how and is embarrassed to acknowledge that." Or "Jeremy is actually delegating as much as he can given his subordinates' current skill levels; they are frustrated but really cannot handle more than they do." Or maybe "Jeremy is delegating quite a lot, but Frank and Joan have some other ax to grind." Liam may be making matters worse without realizing it by sending Jeremy mixed signals: "Empower your subordinates, but make no mistakes." We don't know for sure; nor does Liam.

Operating from this narrow view, Liam also approached the discussion with a binary framing that leaves both parties with very little room to maneuver: "Jeremy must learn to delegate or we'll lose Frank and Joan—and meanwhile, he'll burn himself out." Last but not least, Liam's framing remained frozen throughout the exchange despite clear signals that Jeremy was not buying the feedback. At no point was Liam processing, let alone addressing, Jeremy's objections. It's no surprise that the meeting ended badly.

The Dangers of Easing In

After they've had a few bad experiences delivering narrowly framed feedback, managers tend to fall back on the

SCRIPTED ESCALATION

Take a look at how quickly a minor point of difference during a feedback discussion can turn into a major disagreement. Jerry starts the conversation by noting that he'd done a good job on his project. Beth, his boss, is not in violent disagreement with his assessment and acknowledges that "it wasn't bad." Jerry could reaffirm his opening bid but instead tries to pull Beth's view closer to his own by overstating his initial point. Beth disagrees with Jerry's inflated statement, and instead of reiterating her first comment, she yields to the temptation to pull Jerry closer to her point of view. Both present stronger and stronger positions, trying to convince the other, and a minor difference quickly becomes a major point of contention.

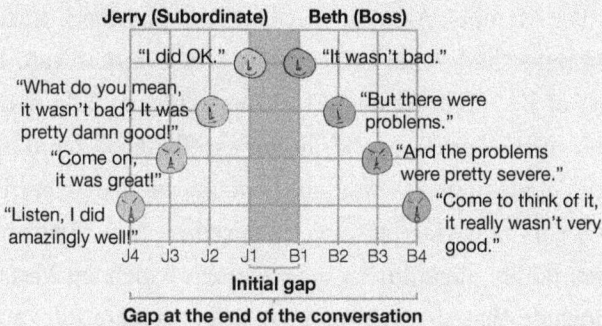

Jerry (Subordinate)   Beth (Boss)

"I did OK."   "It wasn't bad."

"What do you mean, it wasn't bad? It was pretty damn good!"   "But there were problems."

"Come on, it was great!"   "And the problems were pretty severe."

"Listen, I did amazingly well!"   "Come to think of it, it really wasn't very good."

J4   J3   J2   J1   B1   B2   B3   B4

Initial gap

Gap at the end of the conversation

conventional wisdom that it's better to soften bad news with some good.

They try to avoid uncomfortable confrontations by using an indirect approach: They make up their minds about an issue and then try to help their employees reach the same conclusions by asking a carefully designed set of questions.

At first glance, this type of "easing in" seems more open and fair than the forthright approach that Liam took, since the manager is involving the subordinate in a conversation, however scripted. But like the forthright approach, easing in reflects a narrow and binary framing that typically remains frozen throughout the process. Indeed, there would be no need to ease in if the manager were approaching the conversation with a truly open mind. And easing in carries an additional risk: The employee may not give you the answers you're looking for.

For example, Alex, an executive at a pharmaceuticals company, had some difficult news to communicate to one of his subordinates, Erin. She was a middle manager at the company and did an excellent job handling her department but was not contributing satisfactorily to a companywide task force chaired by Alex. Erin was remarkably silent during the meetings, which led Alex to conclude that she was too busy to participate fully and had little to offer the group. Alex's solution? Take her off the task force so she could focus on her primary responsibilities. But because he suspected Erin would be hurt or insulted if he suggested she step down, Alex hoped to prompt her to resign from the committee by asking her a series of questions that would make her see she was too busy to continue. Let's look at what happened.

Alex: "Do you sometimes feel as though you're wasting your time in the task force meetings?"

Erin: "No, I learn a lot from the meetings—and from watching the way you run them."

Alex: "But do you find that your mind is on your daily job when you're at committee meetings?"

Erin: "Not really. I hope I haven't given you the impression that I'm not fully committed. I think this is important work, and I'm excited to be a part of it, and I think I have some good ideas to offer."

Alex: "What if you could participate more informally? You could take yourself off the team as a permanent member, but you could continue to receive the agenda and minutes and contribute when your particular area of expertise is required."

Erin: "It sounds like you want me off the committee. Why? I don't think the committee work has undermined my commitment to my real work. I'm making my numbers. Plus, it's a learning opportunity."

Alex: "No, no, I just want to make sure it's something you really want to do."

Erin: "It is."

As you can see, Erin didn't play along. Alex was not ready for a confrontation, so he folded—and lost. He didn't get Erin off the committee, nor did he communicate his view that her committee work was subpar, so he has no way to help her improve her performance. What's more, he introduced a source of stress into their relationship: Erin is likely to have been unsettled by the interaction, as Alex implied some level of dissatisfaction with her performance without telling her what it is.

As in our previous example, Alex's framing of the issue was narrow: "Erin doesn't talk at the meetings, probably because she's overloaded, so the committee is a waste of her time." His framing was also binary; the interaction could be a success only if Erin agreed to get off the committee without losing her motivation for her regular work. And this framing remained frozen because Alex was concentrating on asking the "right" questions and couldn't process anything but the "right" answers.

Meanwhile, Erin may actually benefit from being on the committee, even if she doesn't say much. She learns a lot, and it gives her visibility. And if she can find a way to contribute more, the committee may well benefit from her membership. But by framing the issue the way he did, Alex excluded other possible solutions, any of which may have been more productive for all concerned: Maybe Erin would talk more in the meetings if Alex probed the reasons for her silence and helped her find a way to contribute what may be very valuable insights. And if overwork is indeed an issue, perhaps there are duties Erin might give up to gain more time and energy.

Easing in is a gamble. You might get lucky, but you have only half the cards. The subordinate may not give you the answers you're looking for, as we saw with Erin, either because she genuinely doesn't agree or because she sees that the game is rigged and refuses to play along. Or the subordinate may decide to stop resisting and pretend to go along but still fail to believe the feedback. And there's another risk, regardless of how the conversation ends: The employee may forever lose confidence in his or her boss. Erin may always wonder what Alex has up his sleeve, having caught him being disingenuous once.

Indeed, that's what happened to Mark, a marketing director at a large consulting firm. His boss, Rene, had called him into a meeting to discuss his role, and Mark left the meeting having relinquished control of his pet project, developing and implementing the company's first advertising campaign. Rene had asked him a series of seemingly innocuous questions, such as "Do you find endless meetings with different agencies to be a waste of your time?" and "Do you feel like your time would be better spent developing new communications materials?" Mark eventually accepted what was clearly the "right" conclusion from his boss's perspective—to surrender the project—even though he wanted to continue. Worse, he didn't know why Rene wanted him off the project, so as a learning opportunity, it was wasted. His relationship with his boss is now tainted; Mark can no longer take Rene's comments at face value.

Why Is It So Hard?

It's very clear from a distance what went wrong for Liam and Alex. Most managers today are well trained and well meaning; why can't they see what they're doing wrong? The tendency to frame threatening situations in narrow terms can be traced to the combination of several phenomena.

First, research shows that when analyzing others' behavior, most people tend to overestimate the effect of a person's stable characteristics—the individual's disposition and capabilities—and underestimate the impact of the specific conditions under which that person is operating. So, for instance, a manager will attribute a subordinate's performance problems to his or her disposition rather than to circumstances in the workplace, leading to a rather simplistic interpretation. This phenomenon is known as the *fundamental attribution error.*

Second, people are more prone to committing the fundamental attribution error when they operate under demanding conditions. We can better distinguish the impact of situational forces when we have time and energy to spare than when we face multiple demands on our attention. Unfortunately, managers tend to be busy. Facing huge workloads and tight deadlines, they have limited time and attention to engage in exhaustive analyses of all the potential causes of the situations they observe or of the many possible solutions to a given problem. So they settle on the first acceptable explanation. "Jeremy's too controlling" explained all the symptoms, so Liam did not go further.

Research can also give us some insight into why bosses tend to frame things in a binary way. In particular, Harvard Business School professor Chris Argyris's work over nearly five decades has established that under stressful circumstances, people behave in predictable ways. They design their behaviors, often unconsciously, to gain control of a situation and to win—which means, unfortunately, that the other side usually has to lose. That's binary framing.

And why is it so hard for bosses to revise their restrictive framing midstream? For several powerful reasons. First, bosses don't set out to frame situations in restrictive ways; they do so unconsciously, most of the time, and it's hard to question a constraint that we don't know we're imposing on ourselves. Second, humans tend to assume that other reasonable people will see the situation as they see it. That's called the *false consensus effect*. Our framing of an issue represents our view of reality, the facts as we see them. We are reasonable and competent people; why would others see the situation differently?

Bosses can get past these hurdles by recognizing them and becoming more conscious and careful when framing decisions. But then they have to beat another cause of frozen framing: a busy processor. For instance, Liam becomes increasingly stressed as Jeremy continues to push back against his version of the facts, and both devote so much energy to trying to control their growing irritation that they have few resources left to listen, process, and respond constructively.

Reframing Feedback

Let's be clear: I'm not suggesting that bosses systematically misdiagnose the causes of their subordinates' performance problems. Liam's and Alex's early diagnoses may well have been right. And even if their feedback discussions had been more productive, their subordinates may not have been able to sufficiently improve their performances to meet their bosses' expectations. But Jeremy and Erin will almost certainly fail to improve if they don't understand and accept the feedback. Restrictive framing not only makes feedback conversations more stressful than they need to be, it also increases the likelihood that subordinates won't believe what their bosses say. Indeed, subordinates are more likely to accept and act on their bosses' feedback if they feel it is developed and communicated fairly. (See the sidebar "Making Feedback More Acceptable.")

So, for instance, imagine how differently Liam and Jeremy's conversation might have gone had the manager framed his concerns more broadly: "I've heard complaints that Jeremy isn't delegating—and some of his employees are feeling sufficiently frustrated that I'm afraid we'll start losing them. I'd like to find out if Jeremy knows about the complaints and get his take on the situation."

This frame isn't narrow. Liam hasn't reached a conclusion about why Jeremy doesn't delegate or whether, indeed, Jeremy is refusing to delegate at all. Nor is the frame binary. Liam hasn't fixed on a win-or-lose outcome. And because Liam hasn't entered the conversation with a preconceived outcome in mind, he has nothing on which to freeze. Now, Liam can open the conversation in a much more open way. He might say, for instance, "Jeremy, I don't know if you're aware of this—or if it's true or not—but I've heard that Frank and Joan are anxious to take on a bit more responsibility. What do you think?" This can lead to a discussion of Frank's and Joan's capabilities, as well as Jeremy's own role and aspirations, without locking Jeremy and Liam into a test of wills.

As for Alex, instead of approaching the meeting with the goal of getting Erin off the committee with minimal

MAKING FEEDBACK MORE ACCEPTABLE

Research shows that people tend to be more willing to accept feedback when they have the feeling that:

- The person offering the feedback is reliable and has good intentions toward them.

- The feedback development process is fair—that is, the person giving the feedback collects all relevant information; allows the subordinate to clarify and explain matters; considers the subordinate's opinions; and applies consistent standards when delivering criticism.

- The feedback communication process is fair— that is, the person offering the feedback pays careful attention to the subordinate's ideas; shows respect for the subordinate; and supports the subordinate despite their disagreements.

This short list makes clear the negative impact of approaching a feedback discussion with restrictive framing: Narrow framing tells the employee that the feedback wasn't developed fairly. And a boss constrained by a binary and frozen frame comes across as biased, close-minded, and unsupportive—ensuring that the subordinate will feel as though the feedback hasn't been communicated fairly.

damage, he could have framed the interaction more broadly: "I have a great subordinate who doesn't say much on the committee. Let's sit down and talk about her work, the committee, her career plans, and how committee membership fits in with those plans." Because this framing doesn't fix on a win-or-lose outcome, Alex would have felt less need to control the discussion and hence less compelled to ease in.

While most managers can easily see what they're doing wrong when shown how they've developed and presented their feedback, restrictive framing remains a surprisingly persistent problem, even for seasoned managers who excel at other aspects of leadership. But giving feedback doesn't have to be stressful for you, demoralizing for your employees, or damaging to your professional relationships.

Offering more effective critiques requires that you learn to recognize the biases that color the development of feedback. It requires that you take the time to consider alternative explanations for behaviors you've witnessed rather than leaping to hasty conclusions that only serve to paint you and your subordinates into a corner. And it requires that you take into account the circumstances an employee is working under rather than attributing weak performance to the person's disposition.

In short, it requires a broad and flexible approach, one that will convince your employees that the process is fair and that you're ready for an honest conversation.

Jean-François Manzoni is Professor of Management Practice and the Shell Chaired Professor in Human Resources and Organisational Development at INSEAD (Singapore campus). He is a coauthor, along with Jean-Louis Barsoux, of *The Set-Up-to-Fail Syndrome: How Good Managers Cause Great People to Fail* (Harvard Business School Press, 2002).

Chapter 5
The Set-Up-to-Fail Syndrome

**by Jean-François Manzoni and
Jean-Louis Barsoux**

A summary of the full-length HBR article by Jean-François
Manzoni and Jean-Louis Barsoux, highlighting key ideas.

IDEA IN BRIEF

That darned employee! His performance keeps deteriorating—*despite* your close monitoring. What's going on?

Brace yourself: You may be at fault, by unknowingly
triggering the set-up-to-fail syndrome. Employees whom
you (perhaps falsely) view as weak performers live *down*
to your expectations. Here's how:

Reprinted from *Harvard Business Review*, March–April 1998 (product
#R98209)

1. You start with a positive relationship.

2. Something—a missed deadline, a lost client—makes you question the employee's performance. You begin micromanaging him.

3. Suspecting your reduced confidence, the employee starts doubting *himself.* He stops giving his best, responds mechanically to your controls, and avoids decisions.

4. You view his new behavior as additional proof of mediocrity—and tighten the screws further.

Why not just fire him? Because you're likely to repeat the pattern with others. Better to *reverse* the dynamic instead. Unwinding the set-up-to-fail spiral actually pays big dividends: Your company gets the best from your employees—and from you.

IDEA IN PRACTICE

How Set-Up-to-Fail Starts

A manager categorizes employees as "in" or "out," based on:

- Early *perceptions* of employees' motivation, initiative, creativity, strategic perspectives

- Previous bosses' impressions

- An early mishap

- Boss-subordinate incompatibility

The manager then notices *only* evidence supporting his categorization, while dismissing contradictory evidence. The boss also treats the groups differently:

- "In" groups get autonomy, feedback, and expressions of confidence.

- Members of "out" groups get controlling, formal management emphasizing rules.

The Costs of Set-Up-to-Fail

This syndrome hurts everyone:

- *Employees* stop volunteering ideas and information and asking for help, avoid contact with bosses, or grow defensive.

- The *organization* fails to get the most from employees.

- The *boss* loses energy to attend to other activities. His reputation suffers as other employees deem him unfair.

- *Team spirit* wilts as targeted performers are alienated and strong performers are overburdened.

How to Reverse Set-Up-to-Fail

If the syndrome hasn't started, prevent it:

- Establish expectations with new employees early. Loosen the reins as they master their jobs.

- Regularly challenge your own assumptions. Ask: "What are the *facts* regarding this employee's performance?" "Is he really that bad?"

- Convey openness, letting employees challenge your opinions. They'll feel comfortable discussing their performance and relationship with you.

If the syndrome has already erupted, discuss the dynamic with the employee:

1. Choose a neutral, nonthreatening location; use affirming language ("Let's discuss our relationship and roles"); and acknowledge your part in the tension.

2. Agree on the employee's weaknesses and strengths. Support assessments with facts, not feelings.

3. Unearth causes of the weaknesses. Do you disagree on priorities? Does your employee lack specific knowledge or skills? Ask: "How is my behavior making things worse for you?"

4. Identify ways to boost performance. Training? New experiences? Decide the quantity and type of supervision you'll provide. Affirm your desire to improve matters.

5. Agree to communicate more openly: "Next time I do something that communicates low expectations, can you let me know immediately?"

When an employee fails—or even just performs poorly—managers typically do not blame themselves. The employee doesn't understand the work, a manager might contend. Or the employee isn't driven to succeed, can't set priorities, or won't take direction. Whatever the reason, the problem is assumed to be the employee's fault— and the employee's responsibility.

But is it? Sometimes, of course, the answer is yes. Some employees are not up to their assigned tasks and never will be, for lack of knowledge, skill, or simple desire. But sometimes—and we would venture to say often—an employee's poor performance can be blamed largely on his boss.

Perhaps "blamed" is too strong a word, but it is directionally correct. In fact, our research strongly suggests that bosses—albeit accidentally and usually with the best intentions—are often complicit in an employee's lack of success. (See the sidebar "About the Research.") How? By creating and reinforcing a dynamic that essentially sets up perceived underperformers to fail. If the Pygmalion effect describes the dynamic in which an individual lives up to great expectations, the set-up-to-fail syndrome explains the opposite. It describes a dynamic in which employees perceived to be mediocre or weak performers live down to the low expectations their managers have for them. The result is that they often end up leaving the organization—either of their own volition or not.

The syndrome usually begins surreptitiously. The initial impetus can be performance related, such as when an employee loses a client, undershoots a target, or misses a deadline. Often, however, the trigger is less specific. An employee is transferred into a division with a lukewarm recommendation from a previous boss. Or perhaps the

ABOUT THE RESEARCH

This article is based on two studies designed to under-stand better the causal relationship between lead-ership style and subordinate performance—in other words, to explore how bosses and subordinates mu-tually influence each other's behavior. The first study, which comprised surveys, interviews, and observa-tions, involved 50 boss-subordinate pairs in four man-ufacturing operations in *Fortune* 100 companies. The second study, involving an informal survey of about 850 senior managers attending INSEAD executive-development programs over the last three years, was done to test and refine the findings generated by the first study. The executives in the second study repre-sented a wide diversity of nationalities, industries, and personal backgrounds.

boss and the employee don't really get along on a personal basis—several studies have indeed shown that compat-ibility between boss and subordinate, based on similarity of attitudes, values, or social characteristics, can have a significant impact on a boss's impressions. In any case, the syndrome is set in motion when the boss begins to worry that the employee's performance is not up to par.

The boss then takes what seems like the obvious ac-tion in light of the subordinate's perceived shortcom-ings: he increases the time and attention he focuses on the employee. He requires the employee to get approval before making decisions, asks to see more paperwork documenting those decisions, or watches the employee at meetings more closely and critiques his comments more intensely.

These actions are intended to boost performance and prevent the subordinate from making errors. Unfortunately, however, subordinates often interpret the heightened supervision as a lack of trust and confidence. In time, because of low expectations, they come to doubt their own thinking and ability, and they lose the motivation to make autonomous decisions or to take any action at all. The boss, they figure, will just question everything they do—or do it himself anyway.

Ironically, the boss sees the subordinate's withdrawal as proof that the subordinate is indeed a poor performer. The subordinate, after all, isn't contributing his ideas or energy to the organization. So what does the boss do? He increases his pressure and supervision again—watching, questioning, and double-checking everything the subordinate does. Eventually, the subordinate gives up on his dreams of making a meaningful contribution. Boss and subordinate typically settle into a routine that is not really satisfactory but, aside from periodic clashes, is otherwise bearable for them. In the worst-case scenario, the boss's intense intervention and scrutiny end up paralyzing the employee into inaction and consume so much of the boss's time that the employee quits or is fired.

Perhaps the most daunting aspect of the set-up-to-fail syndrome is that it is self-fulfilling and self-reinforcing— it is the quintessential vicious circle. The process is self-fulfilling because the boss's actions contribute to the very behavior that is expected from weak performers. It is self-reinforcing because the boss's low expectations, in being fulfilled by his subordinates, trigger more of the same behavior on his part, which in turn triggers more of the same behavior on the part of subordinates. And on and on, unintentionally, the relationship spirals downward.

A case in point is the story of Steve, a manufacturing supervisor for a *Fortune* 100 company. When we first met Steve, he came across as highly motivated, energetic, and enterprising. He was on top of his operation, monitoring problems and addressing them quickly. His boss expressed great confidence in him and gave him an excellent performance rating. Because of his high performance, Steve was chosen to lead a new production line considered essential to the plant's future.

In his new job, Steve reported to Jeff, who had just been promoted to a senior management position at the plant. In the first few weeks of the relationship, Jeff periodically asked Steve to write up short analyses of significant quality-control rejections. Although Jeff didn't really explain this to Steve at the time, his request had two major objectives: to generate information that would help both of them learn the new production process, and to help Steve develop the habit of systematically performing root cause analysis of quality-related problems. Also, being new on the job himself, Jeff wanted to show his own boss that he was on top of the operation.

Unaware of Jeff's motives, Steve balked. Why, he wondered, should he submit reports on information he understood and monitored himself? Partly due to lack of time, partly in response to what he considered interference from his boss, Steve invested little energy in the reports. Their tardiness and below-average quality annoyed Jeff, who began to suspect that Steve was not a particularly proactive manager. When he asked for the reports again, he was more forceful. For Steve, this merely confirmed that Jeff did not trust him. He withdrew more and more from interaction with him, meeting his demands with increased passive resistance. Before long, Jeff became convinced that Steve was not effective enough and couldn't handle his job without help. He started to supervise Steve's every move—to Steve's predictable dismay. One year after excitedly taking on the new production line, Steve was so dispirited he was thinking of quitting.

How can managers break the set-up-to-fail syndrome? Before answering that question, let's take a closer look at the dynamics that set the syndrome in motion and keep it going.

Deconstructing the Syndrome

We said earlier that the set-up-to-fail syndrome usually starts surreptitiously—that is, it is a dynamic that usually creeps up on the boss and the subordinate until suddenly both of them realize that the relationship has gone sour. But underlying the syndrome are several assumptions about weaker performers that bosses appear to accept uniformly. Our research shows, in fact, that executives typically compare weaker performers with stronger performers using the following descriptors:

- Less motivated, less energetic, and less likely to go beyond the call of duty

- More passive when it comes to taking charge of problems or projects

- Less aggressive about anticipating problems

- Less innovative and less likely to suggest ideas

- More parochial in their vision and strategic perspective

- More prone to hoard information and assert their authority, making them poor bosses to their own subordinates

It is not surprising that on the basis of these assumptions, bosses tend to treat weaker and stronger performers very differently. Indeed, numerous studies have shown that up to 90% of all managers treat some subordinates as though they were members of an in-group, while they consign others to membership in an out-group. Members of the in-group are considered the trusted collaborators and therefore receive more autonomy, feedback, and expressions of confidence from their bosses. The boss-subordinate relationship for this group is one of mutual trust and reciprocal influence. Members of the out-group, on the other hand, are regarded more as hired hands and are managed in a more formal, less personal way, with more emphasis on rules, policies, and authority. (For more on how bosses treat weaker and stronger performers differently, see the chart "In with the In Crowd, Out with the Out.")

Why do managers categorize subordinates into either in-groups or out-groups? For the same reason that we

In with the in crowd, out with the out

Boss's behavior toward perceived stronger performers	Boss's behavior toward perceived weaker performers
Discusses project objectives, with a limited focus on project implementation. Gives subordinate the freedom to choose his own approach to solving problems or reaching goals.	Is directive when discussing tasks and goals. Focuses on what needs get done as well as how it should get done.
Treats unfavorable variances, mistakes, or incorrect judgments as learning opportunities.	Pays close attention to unfavorable variances, mistakes, or incorrect judgments.
Makes himself available, as in "Let me know if I can help." Initiates casual and personal conversations.	Makes himself available to subordinate on a need-to-see basis. Bases conversations primarily on work-related topics.
Is open to subordinate's suggestions and discusses them with interest.	Pays little interest to subordinate's comments or suggestions about how and why work is done.
Gives subordinate interesting and challenging stretch assignments. Often allows subordinate to choose his own assignments.	Reluctantly gives subordinate anything but routine assignments. When handing out assignments, gives subordinate little choice. Monitors subordinate heavily.
Solicits opinions from subordinate on organizational strategy, execution, policy, and procedures.	Rarely asks subordinate for input about organizational or work-related matters.
Often defers to subordinate's opinion in disagreements.	Usually imposes own views in disagreements.
Praises subordinate for work well done.	Emphasizes what the subordinate is doing poorly.

tend to typecast our family, friends, and acquaintances: it makes life easier. Labeling is something we all do, because it allows us to function more efficiently. It saves time by providing rough-and-ready guides for interpreting events and interacting with others. Managers, for instance, use categorical thinking to figure out quickly who should get what tasks. That's the good news.

The downside of categorical thinking is that in organizations it leads to premature closure. Having made up his mind about a subordinate's limited ability and poor motivation, a manager is likely to notice supporting evidence while selectively dismissing contrary evidence. (For example, a manager might interpret a terrific new product idea from an out-group subordinate as a lucky onetime event.) Unfortunately for some subordinates, several studies show that bosses tend to make decisions about in-groups and out-groups even as early as five days into their relationships with employees.

Are bosses aware of this sorting process and of their different approaches to "in" and "out" employees? Definitely. In fact, the bosses we have studied, regardless of nationality, company, or personal background, were usually quite conscious of behaving in a more controlling way with perceived weaker performers. Some of them preferred to label this approach as "supportive and helpful." Many of them also acknowledged that—although they tried not to—they tended to become impatient with weaker performers more easily than with stronger performers. By and large, however, managers are aware of the controlling nature of their behavior toward perceived weaker performers. For them, this behavior is not an error in implementation; it is intentional.

What bosses typically do *not* realize is that their tight controls end up hurting subordinates' performance by undermining their motivation in two ways: first, by depriving subordinates of autonomy on the job and, second, by making them feel undervalued. Tight controls are an indication that the boss assumes the subordinate can't perform well without strict guidelines. When the subordinate senses these low expectations, it can undermine his self-confidence. This is particularly problematic because numerous studies confirm that people perform up or down to the levels their bosses expect from them or, indeed, to the levels they expect from themselves.[1]

Of course, executives often tell us, "Oh, but I'm very careful about this issue of expectations. I exert more control over my underperformers, but I make sure that it does not come across as a lack of trust or confidence in their ability." We believe what these executives tell us. That is, we believe that they do try hard to disguise their intentions. When we talk to their subordinates, however, we find that these efforts are for the most part futile. In fact, our research shows that most employees can—and do—"read their boss's mind." In particular, they know full well whether they fit into their boss's in-group or out-group. All they have to do is compare how they are treated with how their more highly regarded colleagues are treated.

Just as the boss's assumptions about weaker performers and the right way to manage them explains his complicity in the set-up-to-fail syndrome, the subordinate's assumptions about what the boss is thinking explain his own complicity. The reason? When people perceive disapproval, criticism, or simply a lack of confidence and appreciation, they tend to shut down—a behavioral phenomenon that manifests itself in several ways.

Primarily, shutting down means disconnecting intellectually and emotionally. Subordinates simply stop giving their best. They grow tired of being overruled, and they lose the will to fight for their ideas. As one subordinate put it, "My boss tells me how to execute every detail. Rather than arguing with him, I've ended up wanting to say, 'Come on, just tell me what you want me to do, and I'll go do it.' You become a robot." Another perceived weak performer explained, "When my boss tells me to do something, I just do it mechanically."

Shutting down also involves disengaging personally—essentially reducing contact with the boss. Partly, this disengagement is motivated by the nature of previous exchanges that have tended to be negative in tone. As one subordinate admitted, "I used to initiate much more contact with my boss until the only thing I received was negative feedback; then I started shying away."

Besides the risk of a negative reaction, perceived weaker performers are concerned with not tainting their images further. Following the often-heard aphorism "Better to keep quiet and look like a fool than to open your mouth and prove it," they avoid asking for help for fear of further exposing their limitations. They also tend to volunteer less information—a simple "heads up" from a perceived underperformer can cause the boss to overreact and jump into action when none is required. As one perceived weak performer recalled, "I just wanted to let my boss know about a small matter, only slightly out of the routine, but as soon as I mentioned it, he was all over my case. I should have kept my mouth closed. I do now."

Finally, shutting down can mean becoming defensive. Many perceived underperformers start devoting more energy to self-justification. Anticipating that they will be personally blamed for failures, they seek to find excuses early. They end up spending a lot of time looking in the rearview mirror and less time looking at the road ahead. In some cases—as in the case of Steve, the manufacturing supervisor described earlier—this defensiveness can lead to noncompliance or even systematic opposition to the boss's views. While this idea of a weak subordinate going head to head with his boss may seem irrational, it may reflect what Albert Camus once observed: "When deprived of choice, the only freedom left is the freedom to say no."

The Syndrome Is Costly

There are two obvious costs of the set-up-to-fail syndrome: the emotional cost paid by the subordinate and the organizational cost associated with the company's failure to get the best out of an employee. Yet there are other costs to consider, some of them indirect and long term.

The boss pays for the syndrome in several ways. First, uneasy relationships with perceived low performers often sap the boss's emotional and physical energy. It can be quite a strain to keep up a facade of courtesy and pretend everything is fine when both parties know it is not. In addition, the energy devoted to trying to fix these relationships or improve the subordinate's performance through increased supervision prevents the boss from attending to other activities—which often frustrates or even angers the boss.

Furthermore, the syndrome can take its toll on the boss's reputation, as other employees in the organization observe his behavior toward weaker performers. If the boss's treatment of a subordinate is deemed unfair or unsupportive, observers will be quick to draw their lessons. One outstanding performer commented on his boss's controlling and hypercritical behavior toward another subordinate: "It made us all feel like we're expendable." As organizations increasingly espouse the virtues of learning and empowerment, managers must cultivate their reputations as coaches, as well as get results.

The set-up-to-fail syndrome also has serious consequences for any team. A lack of faith in perceived weaker performers can tempt bosses to overload those whom they consider superior performers; bosses want to entrust critical assignments to those who can be counted on to deliver reliably and quickly and to those who will go beyond the call of duty because of their strong sense of shared fate. As one boss half-jokingly said, "Rule number one: if you want something done, give it to someone who's busy—there's a reason why that person is busy."

An increased workload may help perceived superior performers learn to manage their time better, especially as they start to delegate to their own subordinates more effectively. In many cases, however, these performers simply absorb the greater load and higher stress which, over time, takes a personal toll and decreases the attention they can devote to other dimensions of their jobs, particularly those yielding longer-term benefits. In the worst-case scenario, overburdening strong performers can lead to burnout.

Team spirit can also suffer from the progressive alienation of one or more perceived low performers. Great teams share a sense of enthusiasm and commitment to a common mission. Even when members of the boss's out-group try to keep their pain to themselves, other team members feel the strain. One manager recalled the discomfort experienced by the whole team as they watched their boss grill one of their peers every week. As he explained, "A team is like a functioning organism. If one member is suffering, the whole team feels that pain."

In addition, alienated subordinates often do not keep their suffering to themselves. In the corridors or over lunch, they seek out sympathetic ears to vent their recriminations and complaints, not only wasting their own time but also pulling their colleagues away from productive work. Instead of focusing on the team's mission, valuable time and energy is diverted to the discussion of internal politics and dynamics.

Finally, the set-up-to-fail syndrome has consequences for the subordinates of the perceived weak performers. Consider the weakest kid in the school yard who gets pummeled by a bully. The abused child often goes home and pummels his smaller, weaker siblings. So it is with the people who are in the boss's out-group. When they have to manage their own employees, they frequently replicate the behavior that their bosses show to them. They fail to recognize good results or, more often, supervise their employees excessively.

Breaking Out Is Hard to Do

The set-up-to-fail syndrome is not irreversible. Subordinates can break out of it, but we have found that to be rare. The subordinate must consistently deliver such superior results that the boss is forced to change the employee from out-group to in-group status—a phenomenon made difficult by the context in which these subordinates operate. It is hard for subordinates to impress their bosses when they must work on unchallenging tasks, with no autonomy and limited resources; it is also hard for them to persist and maintain high standards when they receive little encouragement from their bosses.

Furthermore, even if the subordinate achieves better results, it may take some time for them to register with the boss because of his selective observation and recall. Indeed, research shows that bosses tend to attribute the good things that happen to weaker performers to external factors rather than to their efforts and ability (while the opposite is true for perceived high performers: successes tend to be seen as theirs, and failures tend to be attributed to external uncontrollable factors). The subordinate will therefore need to achieve a string of successes in order to have the boss even contemplate revising the initial categorization. Clearly, it takes a special kind of courage, self-confidence, competence, and persistence on the part of the subordinate to break out of the syndrome.

Instead, what often happens is that members of the out-group set excessively ambitious goals for themselves to impress the boss quickly and powerfully—promising to hit a deadline three weeks early, for instance, or attacking six projects at the same time, or simply attempting to handle a large problem without help. Sadly, such superhuman efforts are usually just that. And in setting goals so high that they are bound to fail, the subordinates also come across as having had very poor judgment in the first place.

The set-up-to-fail syndrome is not restricted to incompetent bosses. We have seen it happen to people perceived within their organizations to be excellent bosses. Their mismanagement of some subordinates need not prevent them from achieving success, particularly when they and the perceived superior performers achieve high levels of individual performance. However, those bosses could be even more successful to the team, the organization, and themselves if they could break the syndrome.

Getting It Right

As a general rule, the first step in solving a problem is recognizing that one exists. This observation is especially relevant to the set-up-to-fail syndrome because of its self-fulfilling and self-reinforcing nature. Interrupting the syndrome requires that a manager understand the dynamic and, particularly, that he accept the possibility that his own behavior may be contributing to a subordinate's underperformance. The next step toward cracking the syndrome, however, is more difficult: it requires a carefully planned and structured intervention that takes the form of one (or several) candid conversations meant to bring to the surface and untangle the unhealthy dynamics that define the boss and the subordinate's relationship. The goal of such an intervention is to bring about a sustainable increase in the subordinate's performance while progressively reducing the boss's involvement.

It would be difficult—and indeed, detrimental—to provide a detailed script of what this kind of conversation should sound like. A boss who rigidly plans for this conversation with a subordinate will not be able to engage in real dialogue with him, because real dialogue requires flexibility. As a guiding framework, however, we offer five components that characterize effective interventions. Although they are not strictly sequential steps, all five components should be part of these interventions.

First, the boss must create the right context for the discussion

He must, for instance, select a time and place to conduct the meeting so that it presents as little threat as possible to the subordinate. A neutral location may be more conducive to open dialogue than an office where previous and perhaps unpleasant conversations have taken place. The boss must also use affirming language when asking the subordinate to meet with him. The session should not be billed as "feedback," because such terms may suggest baggage from the past. "Feedback" could also be taken to mean that the conversation will be one-directional, a monologue delivered by the boss to the subordinate. Instead, the intervention should be described as a meeting to discuss the performance of the subordinate, the role of the boss, and the relationship between the subordinate and the boss. The boss might even acknowledge that he feels tension in the relationship and wants to use the conversation as a way to decrease it.

Finally, in setting the context, the boss should tell the perceived weaker performer that he would genuinely like the interaction to be an open dialogue. In particular, he should acknowledge that he may be partially responsible for the situation and that his own behavior toward the subordinate is fair game for discussion.

Second, the boss and the subordinate must use the intervention process to come to an agreement on the symptoms of the problem

Few employees are ineffective in all aspects of their performance. And few—if any—employees desire to do poorly on the job. Therefore, it is critical that the intervention result in a mutual understanding of the specific job responsibilities in which the subordinate is weak. In the case of Steve and Jeff, for instance, an exhaustive sorting of the evidence might have led to an agreement that Steve's underperformance was not universal but instead largely confined to the quality of the reports he submitted (or failed to submit). In another situation, it might be agreed that a purchasing manager was weak when it came to finding offshore suppliers and to voicing his ideas in meetings. Or a new investment professional and his boss might come to agree that his performance was subpar when it came to timing the sales and purchase of stocks, but they might also agree that his financial analysis of stocks was quite strong. The idea here is that before working to improve performance or reduce tension in a relationship, an agreement must be reached about what areas of performance contribute to the contentiousness.

We used the word "evidence" earlier in discussing the case of Steve and Jeff. That is because a boss needs to back up his performance assessments with facts and data—that is, if the intervention is to be useful. They cannot be based on feelings—as in Jeff telling Steve, "I just have the feeling you're not putting enough energy into the reports." Instead, Jeff needs to describe what a good report should look like and the ways in which Steve's reports fall short. Likewise, the subordinate must be allowed—indeed, encouraged—to defend his performance, compare it with colleagues' work, and point out areas in which he is strong. After all, just because it is the boss's opinion does not make it a fact.

Third, the boss and the subordinate should arrive at a common understanding of what might be causing the weak performance in certain areas

Once the areas of weak performance have been identified, it is time to unearth the reasons for those weaknesses. Does the subordinate have limited skills in organizing work, managing his time, or working with others? Is he lacking knowledge or capabilities? Do the boss and the subordinate agree on their priorities? Maybe the subordinate has been paying less attention to a particular dimension of his work because he does not realize its importance to the boss. Does the subordinate become less effective under pressure? Does he have lower standards for performance than the boss does?

It is also critical in the intervention that the boss bring up the subject of his own behavior toward the subordinate and how this affects the subordinate's performance. The boss might even try to describe the dynamics of the set-up-to-fail syndrome. "Does my behavior toward you make things worse for you?" he might ask, or, "What am

I doing that is leading you to feel that I am putting too much pressure on you?"

This component of the discussion also needs to make explicit the assumptions that the boss and the subordinate have thus far been making about each other's intentions. Many misunderstandings start with untested assumptions. For example, Jeff might have said, "When you did not supply me with the reports I asked for, I came to the conclusion that you were not very proactive." That would have allowed Steve to bring his buried assumptions into the open. "No," he might have answered, "I just reacted negatively because you asked for the reports in writing, which I took as a sign of excessive control."

Fourth, the boss and the subordinate should arrive at an agreement about their performance objectives and on their desire to have the relationship move forward

In medicine, a course of treatment follows the diagnosis of an illness. Things are a bit more complex when repairing organizational dysfunction, since modifying behavior and developing complex skills can be more difficult than taking a few pills. Still, the principle that applies to medicine also applies to business: boss and subordinate must use the intervention to plot a course of treatment regarding the root problems they have jointly identified.

The contract between boss and subordinate should identify the ways they can improve on their skills, knowledge, experience, or personal relationship. It should also include an explicit discussion of how much and what type of future supervision the boss will have. No boss, of course, should suddenly abdicate his involvement; it is legitimate for bosses to monitor subordinates' work, particularly when a subordinate has shown limited abilities in one or more facets of his job. From the subordinate's point of view, however, such involvement by the boss is more likely to be accepted, and possibly even welcomed, if the goal is to help the subordinate develop and improve over time. Most subordinates can accept temporary involvement that is meant to decrease as their performance improves. The problem is intense monitoring that never seems to go away.

Fifth, the boss and the subordinate should agree to communicate more openly in the future

The boss could say, "Next time I do something that communicates low expectations, can you let me know immediately?" And the subordinate might say, or be encouraged to say, "Next time I do something that aggravates you or that you do not understand, can you also let me know right away?" Those simple requests can open the door to a more honest relationship almost instantly.

No Easy Answer

Our research suggests that interventions of this type do not take place very often. Face-to-face discussions about a subordinate's performance tend to come high on the list of workplace situations people would rather avoid, because such conversations have the potential to make both parties feel threatened or embarrassed. Subordinates are reluctant to trigger the discussion because they are worried about coming across as thin-skinned or whiny. Bosses tend to avoid initiating these talks because they are concerned about the way the subordinate might react; the discussion could force the boss to make explicit his lack of confidence in the subordinate, in turn putting the subordinate on the defensive and making the situation worse.[2]

As a result, bosses who observe the dynamics of the set-up-to-fail syndrome being played out may be tempted to avoid an explicit discussion. Instead, they will proceed tacitly by trying to encourage their perceived weak performers. That approach has the short-term benefit of bypassing the discomfort of an open discussion, but it has three major disadvantages.

First, a one-sided approach on the part of the boss is less likely to lead to lasting improvement because it focuses on only one symptom of the problem—the boss's behavior. It does not address the subordinate's role in the underperformance.

Second, even if the boss's encouragement were successful in improving the employee's performance, a unilateral approach would limit what both he and the subordinate could otherwise learn from a more up-front handling of the problem. The subordinate, in particular, would not have the benefit of observing and learning from how his boss handled the difficulties in their relationship— problems the subordinate may come across someday with the people he manages.

Finally, bosses trying to modify their behavior in a unilateral way often end up going overboard; they suddenly give the subordinate more autonomy and responsibility than he can handle productively. Predictably, the subordinate fails to deliver to the boss's satisfaction, which leaves the boss even more frustrated and convinced that the subordinate cannot function without intense supervision.

We are not saying that intervention is always the best course of action. Sometimes, intervention is not possible or desirable. There may be, for instance, overwhelming evidence that the subordinate is not capable of doing his job. He was a hiring or promotion mistake, which is best handled by removing him from the position. In other cases, the relationship between the boss and the subordinate is too far gone—too much damage has occurred to repair it. And finally, sometimes bosses are too busy and under too much pressure to invest the kind of resources that intervention involves.

Yet often the biggest obstacle to effective intervention is the boss's mind-set. When a boss believes that a subordinate is a weak performer and, on top of everything else, that person also aggravates him, he is not going to be able to cover up his feelings with words; his underlying convictions will come out in the meeting. That is why preparation for the intervention is crucial. Before even deciding to have a meeting, the boss must separate emotion from reality. Was the situation always as bad as it is now? Is the subordinate really as bad as I think he is? What is the hard evidence I have for that belief? Could there be other factors, aside from performance, that have led me to label this subordinate a weak performer? Aren't there a few things that he does well? He must have displayed above-average qualifications when we decided to hire him. Did these qualifications evaporate all of a sudden?

The boss might even want to mentally play out part of the conversation beforehand. If I say this to the subordinate, what might he answer? Yes, sure, he would say that it was not his fault and that the customer was unreasonable. Those excuses—are they really without merit? Could he have a point? Could it be that, under other circumstances, I might have looked more favorably upon them? And if I still believe I'm right, how can I help the subordinate see things more clearly?

The boss must also mentally prepare himself to be open to the subordinate's views, even if the subordinate challenges him about any evidence regarding his poor performance. It will be easier for the boss to be open if, when preparing for the meeting, he has already challenged his own preconceptions.

Even when well prepared, bosses typically experience some degree of discomfort during intervention meetings. That is not all bad. The subordinate will probably be somewhat uncomfortable as well, and it is reassuring for him to see that his boss is a human being, too.

Calculating Costs and Benefits

As we've said, an intervention is not always advisable. But when it is, it results in a range of outcomes that are uniformly better than the alternative—that is, continued underperformance and tension. After all, bosses who systematically choose either to ignore their subordinates' underperformance or to opt for the more expedient solution of simply removing perceived weak performers are condemned to keep repeating the same mistakes. Finding and training replacements for perceived weak performers is a costly and recurrent expense. So is moni-toring and controlling the deteriorating performance of a disenchanted subordinate. Getting results *in spite of* one's staff is not a sustainable solution. In other words, it makes sense to think of the intervention as an invest-ment, not an expense—with the payback likely to be high.

How high that payback will be and what form it will take obviously depend on the outcome of the interven-tion, which will itself depend not only on the quality of the intervention but also on several key contextual factors: How long has that relationship been spiraling downward? Does the subordinate have the intellectual and emotional resources to make the effort that will be required? Does the boss have enough time and energy to do his part?

We have observed outcomes that can be clustered into three categories. In the best-case scenario, the interven-tion leads to a mixture of coaching, training, job redesign, and a clearing of the air; as a result, the relationship and the subordinate's performance improve, and the costs as-sociated with the syndrome go away or, at least, decrease measurably.

In the second-best scenario, the subordinate's perfor-mance improves only marginally, but because the sub-ordinate received an honest and open hearing from the boss, the relationship between the two becomes more productive. Boss and subordinate develop a better under-standing of those job dimensions the subordinate can do well and those he struggles with. This improved under-standing leads the boss and the subordinate to explore *together* how they can develop a better fit between the job and the subordinate's strengths and weaknesses. That improved fit can be achieved by significantly modifying the subordinate's existing job or by transferring the subordinate to another job within the company. It may even result in the subordinate's choosing to leave the company.

While that outcome is not as successful as the first one, it is still productive; a more honest relationship eases the strain on both the boss and the subordinate, and in turn on the subordinate's subordinates. If the subordinate moves to a new job within the organization that better suits him, he will likely become a stronger performer. His relocation may also open up a spot in his old job for a better performer. The key point is that, having been treated fairly, the subordinate is much more likely to accept the outcome of the process. Indeed, recent studies show that the perceived fairness of a process has a major impact on employees' reactions to its outcomes. (See "Fair Process: Managing in the Knowledge Economy," by W. Chan Kim and Renée Mauborgne, HBR July–August 1997.)

Such fairness is a benefit even in the cases where, despite the boss's best efforts, neither the subordinate's performance nor his relationship with his boss improves significantly. Sometimes this happens: the subordinate truly lacks the ability to meet the job requirements, he has no interest in making the effort to improve, and the boss and the subordinate have both professional and personal differences that are irreconcilable. In those cases, however, the intervention still yields indirect benefits because, even if termination follows, other employees within the company are less likely to feel expendable or betrayed when they see that the subordinate received fair treatment.

Prevention Is the Best Medicine

The set-up-to-fail syndrome is not an organizational fait accompli. It can be unwound. The first step is for the boss to become aware of its existence and acknowledge the possibility that he might be part of the problem. The second step requires that the boss initiate a clear, focused intervention. Such an intervention demands an open exchange between the boss and the subordinate based on the evidence of poor performance, its underlying causes, and their joint responsibilities—culminating in a joint decision on how to work toward eliminating the syndrome itself.

Reversing the syndrome requires managers to challenge their own assumptions. It also demands that they have the courage to look within themselves for causes and solutions before placing the burden of responsibility where it does not fully belong. Prevention of the syndrome, however, is clearly the best option.

In our current research, we examine prevention directly. Our results are still preliminary, but it appears that bosses who manage to consistently avoid the set-up-to-fail syndrome have several traits in common. They do not, interestingly, behave the same way with all subordinates. They are more involved with some subordinates than others—they even monitor some subordinates more than others. However, they do so without disempowering and discouraging subordinates.

How? One answer is that those managers begin by being actively involved with all their employees, gradually reducing their involvement based on improved performance. Early guidance is not threatening to subordinates, because it is not triggered by performance shortcomings; it is systematic and meant to help set the conditions for future success. Frequent contact in the beginning of the relationship gives the boss ample opportunity to communicate with subordinates about priorities, performance measures, time allocation, and even expectations of the type and frequency of communication. That kind of clarity goes a long way toward preventing the dynamic of the set-up-to-fail syndrome, which is so often fueled by unstated expectations and a lack of clarity about priorities.

For example, in the case of Steve and Jeff, Jeff could have made explicit very early on that he wanted Steve to set up a system that would analyze the root causes of quality control rejections systematically. He could have explained the benefits of establishing such a system during the initial stages of setting up the new production line, and he might have expressed his intention to be actively involved in the system's design and early operation. His future involvement might then have decreased in such a way that could have been jointly agreed on at that stage.

Another way managers appear to avoid the set-up-to-fail syndrome is by challenging their own assumptions and attitudes about employees on an ongoing basis. They work hard at resisting the temptation to categorize employees in simplistic ways. They also monitor their own reasoning. For example, when feeling frustrated about a subordinate's performance, they ask themselves, "What are the facts?" They examine whether they are expecting things from the employee that have not been articulated, and they try to be objective about how often and to what extent the employee has really failed. In other words, these bosses delve into their own assumptions and behavior before they initiate a full-blown intervention.

Finally, managers avoid the set-up-to-fail syndrome by creating an environment in which employees feel comfortable discussing their performance and their relationships with the boss. Such an environment is a function of several factors: the boss's openness, his comfort level with having his own opinions challenged, even his sense of humor. The net result is that the boss and the subordinate feel free to communicate frequently and to ask one another questions about their respective behaviors before problems mushroom or ossify.

The methods used to head off the set-up-to-fail syndrome do, admittedly, involve a great deal of emotional investment from bosses—just as interventions do. We believe, however, that this higher emotional involvement is the key to getting subordinates to work to their full potential. As with most things in life, you can only expect to get a lot back if you put a lot in. As a senior executive once said to us, "The respect you give is the respect you get." We concur. If you want—indeed, need—the people in your organization to devote their whole hearts and minds to their work, then you must, too.

NOTES

1. The influence of expectations on performance has been observed in numerous experiments by Dov Eden and his colleagues. See Dov Eden, "Leadership and Expectations: Pygmalion Effects and Other Self-fulfilling Prophecies in Organizations," *Leadership Quarterly,* Winter 1992, vol. 3, no. 4, pp. 271–305.

2. Chris Argyris has written extensively on how and why people tend to behave unproductively in situations they see as threatening or embarrassing. See, for example, *Knowledge for Action: A Guide to Overcoming Barriers to Organizational Change* (San Francisco: Jossey-Bass, 1993).

Jean-François Manzoni is Professor of Management Practice and the Shell Chaired Professor in Human Resources and Organisational Development at INSEAD (Singapore campus). He is a coauthor, along with Jean-Louis Barsoux, of *The Set-Up-to-Fail Syndrome: How Good Managers Cause Great People to Fail* (Harvard Business School Press, 2002).

Jean-Louis Barsoux is a research fellow at INSEAD, where he specializes in organizational behavior. He is the coauthor with Susan C. Schneider of *Managing Across Cultures.*

Chapter 6

How to Give Feedback That Helps People Grow

by Monique Valcour

Over the years, I've asked hundreds of students in my executive education courses what skills they believe are essential for leaders. "The ability to give tough feedback" comes up frequently. But what exactly is "tough feedback"? The phrase connotes bad news, like when you have to tell a team member that they've screwed up on something important. "Tough" also signifies the way we think we need to *act* when giving negative feedback: firm, resolute, and unyielding.

But the word also points to the discomfort some of us experience when giving negative feedback, and to the

Adapted from content posted on hbr.org on August 11, 2015

challenge of doing so in a way that motivates change instead of making the other person feel defensive. Managers fall into a number of common traps. We might be angry at an employee and use the conversation to blow off steam rather than to coach. Or we may delay giving a needed critique because we anticipate that the employee will become argumentative and refuse to accept responsibility. We might try surrounding negative feedback with praise, like disguising a bitter-tasting pill in a spoonful of honey. But this approach is misguided, because we don't want the constructive message to slip by unnoticed. Instead, it's essential to create conditions in which the receiver can take in feedback, reflect on it, and learn from it.

To get a feel for what this looks like in practice, I juxtapose two feedback conversations that occurred following a workplace conflict. MJ Paulitz, a physical therapist in the Pacific Northwest, was treating a hospital patient one day when a fellow staff member paged her. Following procedure, she excused herself and stepped out of the treatment room to respond to the page. The colleague who sent it didn't answer her phone when MJ called, nor had she left a message describing the situation that warranted the page. This happened two more times during the same treatment session. The third time she left her patient to respond to the page, MJ lost her cool and left an angry voicemail message. Upset upon hearing the message, her colleague reported it to their supervisor as abusive.

MJ's first feedback session took place in her supervisor's office. She recalls, "When I went into his office, he had already decided that I was the person at fault, he had all the information he needed, and he wasn't interested in hearing my side of the story. He did not address the three times she pulled me out of patient care. He did not acknowledge that that might have been the fuse that set me off." Her supervisor referred MJ to the human resources department for corrective action. She left seething with a sense of injustice.

MJ describes the subsequent feedback conversation with human resources as transformative. "The woman in HR could see that I had a lot of just-under-the-surface feelings, and she acknowledged them. She said, 'I can only imagine what you're feeling right now. Here you are in my office, in corrective action. If it were me, I might be feeling angry, frustrated, embarrassed . . . Are any of these true for you?' That made a huge difference."

With trust established, MJ was ready to take responsibility for her behavior and commit to changing it. Next, the HR person said, "Now let's talk about how you reacted to those feelings in the moment." She created a space that opened up a genuine dialogue.

The subsequent conversation created powerful learning that has stuck with MJ to this day. "Oftentimes when we're feeling a strong emotion, we go down what the HR person called a 'cowpath,' because it's well worn, very narrow, and always leads to the same place. Let's say you're angry. What do you do? You blow up. It's okay that you feel those things; it's just not okay to blow up. She asked me to think about what I could do to get on a different path."

"The feedback from the HR person helped me learn to find the space between what I'm feeling and the next thing that slides out of my mouth. She gave me the opportunity to grow internally. What made it work was establishing a safe space, trust, and rapport, and then getting down to 'you need to change'—rather than starting with 'you need to change,' which is what my supervisor did. I did need to change; that was the whole point of the corrective action. But she couldn't start there, because I would have become defensive, shut down, and not taken responsibility. I still to this day think that my coworker should have been reprimanded. But I also own my part in it. I see that I went down that cowpath, and I know that I won't do it a second time."

WHAT PEOPLE ARE SAYING ON HBR.ORG

In any feedback session, **the intention of the giver determines how the message is delivered**—the approach, manner, tone, and words used. If there is trust between the giver and the receiver, and consideration and openness, with the giver's sole focus on the receiver's growth, the feedback may still be tough and but also positive.
—Posted by Cindy

When feedback is "tough," it means the giver is not yet ready to deliver it. It is "tough" because it involves behaviors and feelings the giver cannot understand and control.

Feedback should never be "tough" because it needs to be factual and constructive, based on the

process that has led someone to act in a certain way. Asking open-ended questions is a sure way to make it more effective.
—Posted by Michel

One of my all-time workplace pet peeves is bosses who hear a complaint, jump to conclusions, and refuse to even entertain another side of the story.

It's one thing for a manager to have his or her own opinions on what's good performance and what's not and to refuse to debate them. And I can understand a boss taking action, under some circumstances, if multiple customers or coworkers have complained—without necessarily endorsing the substance of their complaints. But **it's flat-out wrong to conclude that someone had in fact done something wrong, just on someone else's say-so.**
—Posted by Jeffrey

The difference in the two sessions MJ described boils down to *coaching*, which deepens self-awareness and catalyzes growth, versus *reprimanding*, which sparks self-protection and avoidance of responsibility. To summarize, powerful, high-impact feedback conversations share the following elements:

- **An intention to help the employee grow.** The point of the discussion is not to simply tell them what they did wrong. The feedback should increase, not drain, the employee's motivation and resources for change. When preparing for a feedback conversation, reflect on what you hope to achieve and on what impact you'd like to have on them, perhaps by doing a short meditation just before the meeting.

- **Openness on the part of the feedback giver.** If you start off feeling uncomfortable and self-protective, your employee will match that energy, and you'll each leave the conversation frustrated with the other person. By remaining open to their point of view, you'll create a high-quality connection that facilitates change.

- **A collaborative mind-set.** Invite the employee into the problem-solving process. Ask questions such as: What ideas do you have? What are you taking away from this conversation? What steps will you take, by when, and how will I know?

Giving developmental feedback that sparks growth is a critical challenge to master, because it can make the difference between an employee who contributes powerfully and positively to the organization and one who feels diminished by the organization and contributes far less. A single conversation can switch an employee on—or shut them down. A true leader sees the raw material for brilliance in every employee and creates the conditions to let it shine, even when the challenge is tough.

———————

Monique Valcour is an executive coach, keynote speaker, and faculty affiliate of ThirdPath Institute. Her coaching, research, and consulting help companies and individuals craft high-performance, meaningful jobs, careers, workplaces, and lives.

Chapter 7
Recognize Good Work in a Meaningful Way

by Christina Bielaszka-DuVernay

Recognition gets great lip service. Ask three managers if they consider it important to recognize the value their teams deliver, and chances are very good that you'll get three positive responses.

But probe a little bit, and you'll discover that the walk is leagues away from the talk.

Manager 1 makes recognition a priority—when he has time to think about it. For Manager 2, recognizing her team means having sandwiches brought in once or twice a quarter for a conference room lunch. Manager 3 is fairly consistent in doling out praise and rewards—

Adapted from content posted on hbr.org on February 29, 2008

too consistent, in fact. The boilerplate language in his thank-you notes and the inevitable $25 gift certificate to a family-style chain restaurant have become an in-joke among his team members, generating eye rolls more than anything else.

For recognition to strengthen your team's performance, say Adrian Gostick and Chester Elton, authors of *The Carrot Principle: How the Best Managers Use Recognition to Engage Their People, Retain Talent, and Accelerate Performance*, it can't be haphazard, generalized to the group, or generic. So what characterizes recognition that actually works?

Deliver Recognition Frequently

Once or twice a quarter won't cut it, as Manager 2 has not yet realized. Research conducted by The Gallup Organization (Washington, DC) found that employees' engagement and motivation are strongly affected by how often they receive recognition for their work.

Three years after the US branch of accounting firm KPMG introduced its recognition program, Encore, the number of employees who agreed with the statement "Taking everything into account, this is a great place to work" rose 20%. In analyzing the program's effectiveness unit by unit, Sylvia Brandes, KPMG's US director of compensation, discovered that units offering their employees less frequent recognition suffered notably higher turnover than units in which recognition was a frequent occurrence.

So how frequently should you let your team members know you recognize and appreciate their efforts? At least once every other week.

We're not talking gold watches here, point out Gostick and Elton. "Managers who earn the most trust and dedication from their people do so with many simple but powerful actions," they write in *The Carrot Principle*. These can include sending them a sincere thank-you note, copying them on a memo praising their performance, or taking a moment in the weekly staff meeting to highlight their actions. To keep yourself on track, Gostick and Elton recommend maintaining a simple recognition scorecard for every employee that notes the date praise was given and for what.

Tie the Message to Organizational Values

If you want recognition to reinforce the sort of thinking and behavior you'd like to see more of, connect your praise explicitly to the values of the organization, whether that's the team, the unit, or the company as a whole. If you're making a connection to company values, keep in mind that they may be less than clear to the employee.

"So many companies' mission or values statements go wrong," says Gostick. "Either it's a laundry list or it lauds such feel-good but generic values as hard work, service, innovation, and so on. The result is that no one really knows what values or behaviors really matter."

And even when the values are clearly defined and kept to a manageable number, employees are notorious for ignoring or tuning out the various means by which a company seeks to communicate them. When's the last time you read the entire e-mail update from your CEO? Or resisted the urge to fiddle with your mobile device during a speech about the company's values?

But the moment of personal recognition is one time that the employee is not tuning out. And if this occasion is before a group of her peers, chances are that many of them—particularly if they like and respect her—are also paying attention. So when you single out an individual for praise, whether it's in a one-on-one meeting or before a group, link that person's behavior with the organization's values. For example:

- "Thank you, Peter, for going the extra mile to keep our client happy. As you know, our team is trying to improve its service-renewal scores and this client is one of our biggest accounts, so your actions really mean a lot."

- "That was a great idea to invite the special projects team to our staff meeting. We talk a lot around here about the value of cross-unit collaboration, but we don't always do such a good job of actually doing it! I really appreciate your efforts in this area—thanks."

Match the Award to the Achievement

Remember Manager 3 and his $25 restaurant gift certificates? His recognition efforts met with derision because he dispensed them without regard to the degree of the employee's effort or achievement. Someone who came in over the weekend to integrate the latest data into an important report would receive the same reward as someone whose three-month-long project unearthed an opportunity to eliminate $50,000 annually in unit expenses.

"It's demotivating to give someone a minor award for a major accomplishment," says Gostick. "It's a slap in the face."

But before you think in purely monetary terms about what would be appropriate for a certain level of achievement, consider the final quality of effective recognition.

Tailor Rewards to the Individual

What's meaningful to one employee versus another can vary significantly. A particularly ambitious employee might really value face time with the CEO or appointment to a high-level project team as recognition for her efforts. A very conscientious employee who always seems to have trouble leaving the office might get more out of an explicit directive to take a day off and take his family to the zoo, courtesy of the company.

Cash awards, say Gostick and Elton, tend not to be as worthwhile as thank-yous, unless they're quite substantial ($1,000 or more). Instead of using the money to buy something special and memorable, most employees just use it to pay bills and quickly forget about its significance.

Don't Forget Teams

Manager 2's mistake was to try to acknowledge individuals' efforts by giving blanket recognition to the group. It's a tactic that's next to useless.

But when your team as a whole achieves goals, recognizing its accomplishments is perfectly appropriate. And don't wait until the particular project is near completion.

"In sports, we don't wait for the team to win before we applaud; we celebrate each incremental step toward victory," says Gostick. "Yet in business, there's this tendency to wait until the project is clearly working well before we celebrate anything."

At the start of a project, "set short-term goals and articulate the reward the team will receive for reaching them," he advises. Each milestone reached presents an occasion to celebrate everyone's contribution to the group effort, reinforce the project's importance, and reignite the team's commitment to working together creatively and collaboratively in pursuit of the end goal.

Whether you're acknowledging the accomplishments of a team or an individual, recognition can be a key motivator toward pushing your direct reports to the next level.

––––––––––––

Christina Bielaszka-DuVernay was the editor of *Harvard Management Update.*

Section 2
Formal Performance Appraisals

Chapter 8
Delivering an Effective Performance Review

by Rebecca Knight

When performance review season arrives, you know the drill. Drag each of your direct reports into a conference room for a one-on-one, hand them an official-looking document, and then start in with the same, tired conversation. Say some positive things about what the employee is good at, then some unpleasant things about what he's not good at, and end—wearing your most solicitous smile—some more ego strokes. The result: a mixed message that leaves even your best employees feeling disappointed.

Adapted from content posted on hbr.org on November 3, 2011

Your formal review sessions with your employees don't need to be so tiresome—or confusing. If you take the right approach, appraisals are an excellent opportunity to keep solid performers moving onward and upward and redirect the poor ones.

What the Experts Say

For many employees, a face-to-face performance review is the most stressful work conversation they'll have all year. For managers, the discussion is just as tense. "What a performance appraisal requires is for one person to stand in judgment of another. Deep down, it's uncomfortable," says Dick Grote, author of *How to Be Good at Performance Appraisals*. Evaluating an employee's job performance should consist of more than an annual chat, according to James Baron, the William S. Beinecke Professor of Management at Yale School of Management. Performance management is a process, he says: "Presumably, you're giving a tremendous amount of real-time feedback, and your employees are people you know well. Hopefully, your relationship can survive candid feedback." No matter what kind of appraisal system your company uses, here are several strategies to help you make performance review season less nerve-racking and more productive.

Set expectations early

The performance review doesn't start with a sit-down in the spare conference room. You must be clear from the outset how you'll evaluate your employees. Grote suggests holding "performance planning" sessions with each of your direct reports at the beginning of the year to discuss that person's goals and your expectations. (See chapter 11, "How to Set and Support Employee Goals.") "You'll see immediate improvement in performance because everyone knows what the boss expects," he says. "And it earns you the right to hold people accountable at the end of the year." Listen carefully to your employees' personal ambitions, as it will inform the way you assess their work. "Oftentimes, managers are evaluating performance without necessarily knowing what that person's career aspirations are. We often assume that everyone wants to be CEO. But that's not always the case," says Baron. Understanding what your direct reports want from their careers will help you figure out ways to broaden their professional experiences.

Lay the groundwork

About two weeks before the face-to-face review, ask your employee to jot down a few things he's done over the last year that he's proud of. This will both help refresh your memory and "put a positive focus on an event that is so often seen as negative," says Grote. Next, review other notes you've kept on him throughout the year: a well-executed project; a deadline missed; the deft handling of a difficult client. Finally, ask for feedback from others in the company who work closely with your employee. "The larger number of independent evaluations the better," says Baron. About an hour before the meeting, give your employee a copy of his appraisal. That way, he can have his initial emotional response—positive or negative—in the privacy of his own cubicle. "When people read someone's assessment of them, they are going to have all sorts of churning emotions," says Grote. "Let them have that on their own time, and give them a chance to think about it." Then with a calmer, cooler head, the employee can prepare for a rational and constructive business conversation.

Set the tone

Too often, the face-to-face conversation takes the form of a "feedback sandwich": compliments, criticism, more praise. But this approach demoralizes your stars and falsely encourages your poor performers. Instead, pick a side. "Most people are good solid workers, so for the vast majority, you should concentrate exclusively on things the person has done well," says Grote, adding that this method tends to motivate people who are already competent at their jobs. For your marginal workers, however, do not sugarcoat bad news. Performance reviews are your chance to confront poor performers and demand improvement. "People are resilient," says Grote. "As time goes on, that person is not going to get a promotion and not going to get a raise . . . You're not doing this person any favors by [avoiding their deficiencies]." (For more on dealing with those who are not meeting expectations, see chapter 14, "How to Help an Underperformer.")

Constructively coach

After discussing the strengths and achievements of your solid performers, ask them how they feel about how things are going. "In most cases, you're dealing with mature adults and you'll elicit their honest concerns," says Grote. For both solid and poor performers, frame feedback in terms of a "stop, start, and continue" model, suggests Baron. What is the employee doing now that is not working? What actions should they adopt to be more successful? What are they doing that is highly effective? Focusing on behaviors, not dispositions, takes the personal edge out of the conversation. Give specific advice and targeted praise. "Don't say things like: 'You need to be more proactive.' That doesn't mean anything. Say something like: 'You need to take more initiative in calling potential sales leads.'" Similarly, "Saying: 'You're an innovator' is nice but it's helpful to know exactly what they're doing that reflects that," says Baron.

Hold your ground

The hot-button issues associated with performance reviews are money and rank. If your company allows it, separate any talk of compensation from the performance review. "But if you must, do not save the salary information for the end of the conversation," says Grote, "otherwise there'll be an invisible parrot above the employee's head squawking: 'How much?' throughout the entire discussion." Rank is another place for potential bruised feelings. A majority of companies require managers to rate their employees—often on a scale of 1 to 5. Your goal is go over the data and make a judgment call. Remember: the 1–5 system is not analogous to the A–F grading scheme in school; most employees will get the middle rank, a 3. This might leave some employees feeling let down, thinking they're merely "average." Don't cave in. "In the corporate world, you're dealing with a highly selective group," says Grote. "The rules of the game have changed. In school, a C was mediocre, but a 3 in the working world means they're meeting expectations. They're shooting par." Conveying that message is a leadership challenge. "People can accept it rationally but it may be hard to accept viscerally," he says. "This is why it's so important to hold a performance planning meeting at the outset. If they hit their targets, they are a 3. It's a goal."

Principles to Remember

- Make it clear at the beginning of the year how you'll evaluate your employees with individual performance planning sessions.

- Give your employees a copy of their appraisal before the meeting so they can have their initial emotional response in private.

- Deliver a positive message to your good performers by concentrating mainly on their strengths and achievements during the conversation.

- Note specific behaviors you want your employee to stop, start, and continue.

Case Study #1: Understand Expectations and Set the Right Tone

Ben Snyder (not his real name), an expat working in London at a global media company, was new at his job. He'd inherited an employee, Jim, whose primary responsibility was to travel to Africa, the Middle East, and Russia to develop partnerships that would ultimately drive sales to Ben's business. But Jim wasn't delivering.

"During quarterly performance reviews, Jim and I had long conversations about his approaches and the great relationships he was developing. I would tell him how glad I was that people were talking to him, that he was forming these relationships. But I also told him that we needed tangible deals," says Ben.

This happened for three straight quarters: same conversation, no deals. Increasingly, Ben was under pressure: Jim was spending a lot of the company's money with nothing to show for it.

"I needed to scare him into action. At the next performance review, I gave Jim 90 days to close a deal."

Nothing changed, and Jim was dismissed. "Even when we sat down with HR and let him go, he was genuinely surprised," recalls Ben.

In retrospect, Ben says he went overboard in validating Jim's spadework, and didn't establish the right tone during their conversations. "The message wasn't clear—Jim only heard what he wanted to hear—the positive praise about the relationship building. He ignored the demand to close deals."

Ben also should have worked harder in the beginning to understand the specifics of Jim's job and set clear expectations. "It was a business I wasn't familiar with. I didn't know how to push him in the right direction because I wasn't exactly sure what he was doing. I had never really sat down with him and defined what success should look like."

Case Study #2: Be Clear and Specific

Lucy Orren (name has been changed) worked as a director of business development at a biotech start-up in New Jersey. She managed Peter, who was, according to Lucy, "a real star. He was smart, very conscientious, and good at everything he tried." One of Peter's biggest responsibilities was giving presentations.

"One of the vice presidents at my company brought it to my attention that Peter used a certain crutch phrase too often, and that while he was a good speaker, he was very deliberate in the way that he spoke, which was sometimes too slow. She thought it connoted a lack of energy. I thought it was a relatively minor problem, but I decided to bring it up in the performance appraisal."

During the face-to-face discussion, however, Lucy chickened out. "Peter was so good at his job, that I was reluctant to give him any criticism," she says. "I tried to couch the advice when we were discussing his strengths. He didn't get it."

At the very end of the conversation, Lucy highlighted areas of improvement. She told Peter to try to be more upbeat during his presentations. But the advice was too vague; Peter wasn't sure what to do with the recommendation.

"The next few presentations he gave were pretty rocky. He overcompensated," recalls Lucy.

After one of his presentations, Lucy realized she needed to be more specific with her coaching. She warned him of the crutch phrase and told him to try to speak faster.

"Peter came through, and improved on every level. He still uses the crutch phrase every so often, but there is more momentum to his presentations."

———————

Rebecca Knight is a freelance journalist in Boston and a lecturer at Wesleyan University. Her work has been published in the *New York Times, USA Today,* and the *Financial Times.*

Chapter 9
Managing Performance When It's Hard to Measure

by Jim Whitehurst

Organizations of all kinds have long struggled to accurately measure the performance of individual members. The typical approach is to assess an individual's performance against a metric usually tied to whether or not they performed a task and the amount of output they generated by doing so. There's a lot riding on these assessments: everything from compensation increases and bonus payments to promotions. And as anyone who has ever given or received a traditional performance review

Adapted from content originally posted on hbr.org on May 11, 2015 knows, this process can be highly subjective—even in the most metrics-obsessed organizations.

But what about the kinds of jobs where measuring someone's "output" isn't about counting the number of widgets they produced, but rather it's about how they managed a team or influenced others or helped people collaborate better? While it might be easy to measure someone's output on an assembly line, how do we decide how well a manager manages or a leader leads?

In the case of an organization like Red Hat (where I am the CEO), which collaborates with many open source software communities like Linux and OpenStack, these questions are all the more difficult to answer—like how to measure someone's contribution to an external community—and traditional performance reviews just don't cut it for us. For example, building enterprise open source software, like we do at Red Hat, involves collaborating with people outside of the company who volunteer their efforts. That means you can't simply issue orders or direct what work gets done and when. What you can do is build influence and trust with other members of the community. But doing that can involve making contributions that offer no direct output or result. It's not quid pro quo, and it's not easy to track and measure.

Conventional performance reviews can also undermine a company's agility and lead to missed opportunities (see the sidebar "Deloitte's Performance Snapshot"). What happens when an individual's goals no longer make sense because the competitive landscape has changed, but their performance rating (and by extension, their compensation and advancement opportunities) is resting on the completion of those goals? That's not a system that promotes innovation.

How do you even begin to appraise someone's performance in these scenarios?

At Red Hat, we've developed a simpler, more flexible approach to performance reviews, one that doesn't limit managers to narrow measures of performance.

Agree on Employee Objectives

We've found that it's essential to ensure that associates and their managers are on the same page when it comes to the responsibilities and expectations for the role. We encourage people to track what's important and to set individual goals that contribute to our company's mission and strategy. We recommend a regular check-in process to keep managers and associates in sync. However, we've found it best to let managers and associates determine the frequency of those meetings. Some take place weekly, others happen on a monthly or quarterly basis.

Get Input from Others

When measuring against these goals, we rely not only on the manager's observations, but also on associates' peers and communities to informally assess how people perform. We pay attention to their reputations and how they are regarded by others. We look at the scope and quality of their influence. The result is that rather than "managing up" to their boss to get a good review, Red Hatters are accountable to the community as a whole.

Focus on Opportunities, Not Score-keeping

Our associates are incredibly talented, passionate people. We don't want them to fixate on a number or letter grade, so we don't hand them a bottom-line score to sum up last year's performance. Instead, we focus on developing their strengths and growing their capabilities. We advise managers to give continuous, real-time feedback throughout the year and to use the annual review as an opportunity to reflect back on everything their associates have achieved, what they've learned along the way, and what opportunities they will pursue in the coming months. Unlike many companies, we don't expect our managers to fit people to a bell curve with a maximum number of low and high performers. Instead, we tell them to pay attention to both performance and potential and to focus on connecting their people with opportunities for growth and development.

DELOITTE'S PERFORMANCE SNAPSHOT

by Marcus Buckingham and Ashley Goodall

At Deloitte we're redesigning our performance management system. Like many other companies, we realize that our current process for evaluating the work of our people—and then training them, promoting them, and paying them accordingly—is increasingly out of step with our objectives.

In a public survey Deloitte conducted recently, more than half the executives questioned (58%) believe that their current performance management approach drives neither employee engagement nor high performance. They, and we, are in need of something nimbler, real-time, and more individualized—something squarely focused on fueling performance in the future rather than assessing it in the past.

What might surprise you, however, is what we'll include in Deloitte's new system and what we won't. It will have no cascading objectives, no once-a-year reviews, and no 360-degree-feedback tools. We've arrived at a very different and much simpler design for managing people's performance. Its hallmarks are speed, agility, one-size-fits-one, and constant learning, and it's underpinned by a new way of collecting reliable performance data.

Rather than asking more people for their opinion of a team member (in a 360-degree or an upward-feedback survey, for example), we found that we will need to ask only the immediate team leader—but, critically, to ask a different kind of question. People may rate other people's skills inconsistently, but they are highly consistent when rating their own feelings and intentions. To see performance at the individual level, then, we will ask team leaders not about the *skills* of each team member

(continued)

(*continued*)

but about their *own future actions* with respect to that person.

At the end of every project (or once every quarter for long-term projects) we will ask team leaders to respond to four future-focused statements about each team member:

1. Given what I know of this person's performance, and if it were my money, I would award this person the highest possible compensation increase and bonus.

2. Given what I know of this person's performance, I would always want him or her on my team.

3. This person is at risk for low performance.

4. This person is ready for promotion today.

In effect, we are asking our team leaders what they would *do* with each team member rather than what they *think* of that individual. When we aggregate these data points over a year, weighting each according to the duration of a given project, we produce a rich stream of information for leaders' discussions of what they, in turn, will do—whether it's a question of succession planning, development paths, or performance-pattern analysis.

In addition to this consistent—and countable—data, when it comes to compensation, we want to factor in some uncountable things, such as the difficulty of project assignments in a given year and contributions to the organization other than formal projects. So the data will serve as the starting point for compensation, not the ending point. The final determination will be reached either by a leader who knows each individual personally or by a group of leaders looking at an entire segment of our practice and at many data points in parallel.

We could call this new evaluation a rating, but it bears no resemblance, in generation or in use, to the ratings of the past. Because it allows us to quickly capture performance at a single moment in time, we call it a *performance snapshot.*

Adapted from "Reinventing Performance Management" (*Harvard Business Review,* April 2015), reprint #R1504B.

Marcus Buckingham provides performance management tools and training to organizations. He is the author of several best-selling books and *StandOut 2.0: Assess Your Strengths, Find Your Edge, Win at Work* (Harvard Business Review Press, 2015).

Ashley Goodall is the director of leader development at Deloitte Services LP, based in New York.

Emphasize Achievement, Not Just Advancement

Finally, when it comes to promotions, raises, and bonuses, we don't force managers to apply a merit matrix or rigid formula. Instead, we give them the flexibility to make decisions that are right for their people. This means our managers don't have to enter inaccurate ratings to "game the system," a problem faced by many other companies.

The conventional way to reward top performers is to promote them into managerial roles. This often creates an army of ineffective and unengaged managers. But we have come to embrace the concept of a "career of achievement" in addition to a "career of advancement." Some of the most influential leaders in our organization do not have fancy titles or even people who directly report to them. They are expert individual contributors who help shape the direction and priorities of Red Hat and key open source communities through their contributions and thought leadership.

A great example is Máirín Duffy, one of our user interface designers. Máirín started working at Red Hat as an intern and later joined us full time in 2005, after she graduated from college. While Máirín has made exceptional contributions to our core Red Hat Enterprise Linux product, she has also earned a stellar reputation throughout the company (as well as open source communities) for her reasoned and intelligent contributions to mailing list conversations on everything from the creation of Red Hat's mission statement to contentious internal debates.

It was in a case involving the latter that led Red Hat's executive vice president and chief people officer DeLisa Alexander to approach Máirín to talk about a proposed project. In other words, a senior leader in the company went directly to someone working closer to the front lines to gather feedback on a fairly major corporatewide decision, simply because DeLisa knew that Máirín could help make or break the success of the final decision based on her level of influence throughout the company.

A traditional performance review rating could never capture the kind of influence Máirín has built inside our organization and the communities we participate in. Even a 360-degree review from her immediate peers or manager wouldn't reach far enough to show Máirín's impact. But everyone at Red Hat knows who Máirín is because her contributions shape many areas of the company. With a performance management process that emphasizes individual development, influence, and innovation, Red Hat is able to retain and grow passionate, talented associates like Máirín.

Jim Whitehurst is the president and CEO of Red Hat, the world's leading provider of open source enterprise IT products and solutions, and the author of the book *The Open Organization* (Harvard Business Review Press, 2015).

Chapter 10
Stop Worrying About Your Employee's Weaknesses

by Peter Bregman

Your son comes home one day, looks down at his feet, and gives you his report card. You smile at him as you open it up and look inside. Then your smile disappears when you see the F in math. You also see an A (English) and two Bs (history and science). You look down at him and ask, "What happened in math, Johnny? Why did you get this F?"

We want our kids to be successful at everything they do. And if they're not good at something, we ask why they failed. We tell them to work harder at it. Understand what went wrong, focus, and fix it.

Adapted from content posted on hbr.org on May 19, 2009

WHAT PEOPLE ARE SAYING ON HBR.ORG

A great manager recognizes the strengths of their people and then puts them in position to win. **A performance review would serve the company better if it were less a report card and more of a coaching session.** The manager should focus on providing the necessary resources to the employee (in your example, someone who loves spreadsheets) and removing the obstacles so that the employee can win. Given that the employee is in the right position, it is often the manager who is the obstacle to success.
—Posted by Ted

This is a terrific approach to managing and motivating employees. If you take it one step further and **share individual members' strengths with the whole team, they begin to see each other for the unique qualities they bring.** They even begin to rely on each other in new ways. And, focusing on strengths lets an employee's gifts shine and productivity climbs and confidence grows.
—Posted by Amy

Some respondents have criticized your example about the salesperson and the spreadsheet. However, **I find that I actually become more proficient in weak areas by partnering with an expert** who will do the work and also explain things to me in terms I can understand.
—Posted by Mary

I'm a presentation skills coach, [and] I always try to coach people to focus on their strengths and build on what they do well. **The more comfortable and confident people get, the more their "weaknesses" will disappear.** People often ask for constructive criticism and want know what they're doing wrong. They're not doing anything "wrong." They can be coached to do something "different" that might compensate for their (temporary) shortcomings.

—Posted by Steve

But that's a mistake. The wrong focus. If you dwell on Johnny's failure, on his weakness, you'll be setting him up for a life of struggle and low self-esteem while reducing his chances of reaching his full potential.

And you won't fix his weakness. You'll just reinforce it.

The problem with a report card is that it measures all students against the same criteria, which ignores that each student is different—with unique talents, distinct likes and dislikes, and particular aspirations. And when we see the F on Johnny's report card, it's easy for us to get distracted from our primary job: to help him deeply enjoy his life and fulfill his potential by developing and deriving pleasure from his unique talents.

Fast-forward 20 years. Johnny is now an adult. As he sits down for a performance review with his manager, she spends a few quiet minutes looking over his review and then raises her eyes to meet his.

"You've worked hard this year, John. Your client orientation is superb. You've met your sales goals, and you're a solid team player. But you have an area that needs development, specifically, your detail orientation. The spreadsheets we get from you are a mess. Let's talk about how you can get better in that."

An A, two Bs, and an F. And his manager handles it the same way his parent did. By focusing the conversation, and John's effort, on his least favorite and weakest area.

We have a report card problem in our companies, and it's costing us a tremendous amount of time, money, potential, and happiness. It's costing us talent.

Traditional management systems encourage mediocrity in everything and excellence in nothing. Most performance-review systems set an ideal picture of how we want everyone to act (standards, competencies, and so on) and then assess how closely people match that ideal, nudging them to improve their weaknesses so they "meet or exceed expectations" in every area.

But how will John add the most value to his organization? He's amazing with people, not spreadsheets. He'll work hardest, derive the most pleasure, and contribute his maximum potential with the greatest result if he is able to focus as much time as possible in his area of strength.

Which means taking his focus off developing the things in which he's weak. They're just a distraction.

Here's what his manager should say: "You've worked hard this year, John. Your client orientation is superb. You've met your sales goals, and you're a solid team player. But working on those spreadsheets isn't a good use of your time, and it's not your strength. I'm going to ask David to do those for you from now on. He loves spreadsheets and is great at them. I want to spend the rest of our time talking about how you can get even better at working with your clients. That's where you shine—where you add the most value to the company—and you seem to really enjoy it."

An organization should be a platform for unique talent. A performance-review system should be flexible enough to reflect and reward the successful contributions of diverse employees. Let's acknowledge that no one can possibly be great at everything—and place all our effort on developing their strengths further.

If it's impossible to take away the part of their job in which they're weak, then help them improve just enough so that it doesn't get in the way of their strength. If you can't take the spreadsheets away from John, help him get a C and move on. That would be preferable to spending the time and effort it would take for him to get an A or even a B.

———————

Peter Bregman is CEO of Bregman Partners, a company that strengthens leadership in people and in organizations through programs (including the Bregman Leadership Intensive), coaching, and as a consultant to CEOs and their leadership teams. Best-selling author of *18 Minutes*, his most recent book is *Four Seconds*.

Chapter 11
How to Set and Support Employee Goals

by Amy Gallo

As you think about how employees should be developing and what their future looks like, you must also think about the goals they should be aspiring to. Employees want to see how their work contributes to larger corporate objectives, and setting the right targets makes this connection explicit for them and for you, their manager.

A performance planning meeting shortly after the review session affords you an opportunity to collaborate with your direct report on goals for the upcoming year, since where your employees need to improve will be fresh on your mind. Within this conversation, you can

Adapted from content posted on hbr.org on February 7, 2011

discuss not only your perception of where your employees should devote their time, but also what they want in their own career and how they're going to reach those milestones.

What the Experts Say

How involved should you be in helping employees establish and achieve their goals? Since failure to meet goals can have consequences for you, your employee, and your team, as well as the broader organization, you need to balance your involvement with the employee's ownership over the process. Linda Hill, coauthor of *Being the Boss: The 3 Imperatives for Becoming a Great Leader,* says, "A manager's job is to provide 'supportive autonomy' that's appropriate to the person's level of capability." The key is to be hands-on while giving your people the room they need to succeed on their own. Here are some principles to follow as you navigate how to best craft goals and support your people in reaching their objectives.

Connect employee goals to larger company goals

For goals to be meaningful and effective in motivating employees, they must be tied to larger organizational ambitions. Employees who don't understand the roles they play in their company's success are more likely to become disengaged. "Achieving goals is often about making trade-offs when things don't go as planned. [Employees] need to understand the bigger picture to make those trade-offs when things go wrong," says Hill. No matter what level the employee is at, they should be able to articulate exactly how their efforts feed into the broader company strategy.

Make goals attainable but challenging

Since employees are ultimately responsible for reaching their goals, they need to have a strong voice in setting them. However, you need to support them through this process by providing input and direction regarding what the company is trying to achieve. Ask your employee to draft goals that directly contribute to the organization's mission. Once they've suggested an initial list, discuss whether the targets are both realistic and challenging enough. "Stretch targets emerge as a process of negotiation between the employee and the manager," says Srikant M. Datar, the Arthur Lowes Dickinson Professor of Accounting at Harvard University. Be careful, though: Your team members are likely to resent you if you insist on goals that are too challenging to accomplish. Don't aim too low, either. If you are overly cautious, you will miss opportunities and settle for mediocrity. "When done well, stretch goals create a lot of energy and momentum in an organization," says Datar. But when done badly, they "do not achieve the goal of motivating employees and helping them achieve better performance as they were designed to do." Even worse, poorly set goals can undermine employees' morale and productivity, and the organization's performance overall.

Create a plan for success

Once a goal is set, ask your employee to explain how they plan to meet it. Have them break it down into tasks and set interim objectives, especially if it's a large or long-term project. Ask your employee: "What are the appropriate milestones?" "What are possible risks, and how do you plan to manage them?" Because targets are rarely pursued in a vacuum, Hill suggests that you "help your people understand who they are dependent on to achieve those goals." Then problem solve with them on how to best influence those people to get the job done.

Monitor progress

Staying on top of employee progress will help head off any troubles early on. "We often get problems because we don't signal that we are partners in achieving goals," says Hill. Don't wait for review time or the end of a project to check in. Review long-term and short-term goals on a weekly basis. Even your high-performing employees need ongoing feedback and coaching. Ask your employee what type of monitoring and feedback would be most helpful to them, especially if the task is particularly challenging or something they are doing for the first time.

Assist in problem solving

Very few of us reach our goals without some bumps along the way. Build relationships with employees so that they feel comfortable coming to you if and when problems arise. If your employee encounters an unforeseen obstacle, the goal may need reworking. First, however, ask them to bring a potential solution to you so you can give them coaching and advice. If their efforts to solve the problem fail, you will need to get further involved.

Sculpt for personal goals

Some managers neglect to think about what an employee is personally trying to accomplish in the context of work.

"If I account for the interests of the whole person, not just the work person, I'm going to get more value from them," says Stewart D. Friedman, author of *Total Leadership: Be a Better Leader, Have a Richer Life.* For example, if your employee has expressed an interest in teaching but that is not part of their job responsibilities, you may be able to find ways to sculpt that job to include opportunities to train peers or less-experienced colleagues. (See the sidebar "Job Sculpting.")

JOB SCULPTING

by Timothy Butler and James Waldroop

Job sculpting is the art of matching people to jobs through a customized career path that allow their deeply embedded life interests to be expressed—and increase the chance of retaining talented people. Since an effective performance review dedicates time to discussing past performance and plans for the future, it presents an opportune time to job sculpt.

Managers don't need special training to job sculpt. They just need to start listening more carefully when employees describe what they like and dislike about

(continued)

(*continued*)

their jobs. Consider the case of a pharmaceutical company executive who managed 30 salespeople. In a performance review, one of her people offhandedly mentioned that her favorite part of the past year had been
helping their division find new office space and negotiating for its lease. In the past, the executive would
have paid the comment little heed. After all, what did
it have to do with the woman's performance in sales?
But listening with the ears of a job sculptor, the executive probed further, asking, "What made the search for
new office space fun for you?" and "How was that different from what you do day-to-day?" The conversation
revealed that the saleswoman was actually very dis-
satisfied and bored with her current position and was
considering leaving. In fact, the saleswoman yearned
for work that met her deeply embedded life interests,
which had to do with *influence through language and
ideas* and *creative production*. Her sales job encom-
passed the former, but it was only when she had the
chance to think about the location, design, and layout
of the new office that her creativity could be fully expressed. The manager helped the woman move to a
position where her primary responsibility was to design
marketing and advertising materials.

Along with listening carefully and asking probing
questions during the performance review, managers

can ask employees to play an active role in job sculpting—before the meeting starts. In most corporate settings, the employee's preparation for a performance review includes a written assessment of accomplishments, goals for the upcoming review period, skill areas in need of development, and plans for accomplishing both goals and growth. During the review, this assessment is then compared to the supervisor's assessment.

But imagine what would happen if employees were also expected to write up their personal views of career satisfaction. Imagine if they were to prepare a few paragraphs on what kind of work they love or if they described their favorite activities on the job. Because so many people are unaware of their deeply embedded life interests—not to mention unaccustomed to discussing them with their managers—such exercises might not come easily at first. Yet they would be an excellent starting point for a discussion, ultimately allowing employees to speak more clearly about what they want from work, both in the short and long term. And that information would make even the best job-sculpting managers more effective.

Once managers and employees have discussed deeply embedded life interests, it's time to customize the next work assignment accordingly. In cases where the employee requires only a small change in his

(continued)

(*continued*)

activities, that might just mean adding a new responsibility. For example, an engineer who has a deeply embedded life interest in *counseling and mentoring* might be asked to plan and manage the orientation of new hires. Or a logistics planner with a deeply embedded life interest in *influence through language and ideas* could be given the task of working on recruitment at college campuses. The goals here would be to give some immediate gratification through an immediate and real change in the job and to begin the process of moving the individual to a role that more fully satisfies him.

Adapted from "Job Sculpting: The Art of Retaining Your Best People" (*Harvard Business Review*, September–October 1999), reprint #99502.

Timothy Butler is Director of Career Development Programs at Harvard Business School and author of *Getting Unstuck: How Dead Ends Become New Paths.*

James Waldroop is a founding principal of the consulting firm Peregrine Partners.

The first step is for you to understand what these goals are. Ask employees if they have any personal goals they want to share with you. Don't pressure them; they should share these aspirations only if they feel comfortable. Friedman suggests you then ask, "What adjustments might we try that would help you achieve your goals?"

This allows the employee to take ownership of the solution. Just as with work goals, you need to be sure personal goals contribute to your team, unit, or to the company. "It's got to be a shared commitment to experiment and mutual responsibility to check in on how it's going. It's got to be a win for both," says Friedman.

Hold people accountable—including yourself

There will be times, even with the best support, when employees fail to meet their targets. Hill advises, "Hold people accountable. You can't say 'Gee, that's too bad.' You need to figure out what went wrong and why." Discuss with your employee what happened and what each of you think went wrong. If the problem was within their control, ask them to apply the possible solutions you've discussed, take another stab at reaching the goal, and check in with you more frequently. If it was something that was outside their power or the goal was too ambitious, acknowledge the disappointment but don't dwell on it. "Do the diagnosis, get the learning, and move on," says Hill.

As discussed in chapter 5, "The Set-Up-to-Fail Syndrome," it's possible that you may have contributed to the problem. Be willing to reflect on your role in the failure. Were you too hands-off, and fail to check in frequently enough? Did you not review the work in a timely way? Have an open conversation about what you can do next time. "If you don't hold yourself accountable, they're going to have trouble with you," says Hill.

Principles to Remember

Do:

- Connect individuals' goals to broader organization objectives

- Show employees that you are a partner in achieving their goals

- Learn about and incorporate employees' personal interests into their professional goals

Don't:

- Allow employees to set goals alone

- Take a hands-off approach with high performers

- Ignore failures

Case Study: A Partner in Goal Attainment

Meghan Lantier is known at Bliss PR for being a natural people developer. As the vice president of the firm's financial services practice, Meghan manages several senior account executives, including Shauna Ellerson (not her real name). Meghan has overseen Shauna's work since Shauna started at Bliss four-and-a-half years ago. Since the beginning, they have set goals through a collaborative process: Shauna develops draft goals, Meghan comes up with goals she believes Shauna needs to focus on, and then they identify the overlap between them. "I want to make sure they are manageable but stretched, too," says Meghan. The two regularly check in on these goals. Meghan takes a hands-on approach, providing Shauna with regular input. They also sit down together at least four times a year to have a more formal discussion about Shauna's ambitions.

One of Shauna's goals is to become more of a thought leader on one of their largest financial services accounts. She has mastered the day-to-day work of managing the client and now needs to focus on the bigger picture. Shauna has been working on this goal for several months now by speaking up more in client meetings and providing more input into the content, not just the process, of their work. "We don't need a goal-review session. I give her constant feedback in the context of the work," says Meghan.

Meghan also knows that, ultimately, Shauna is responsible for her own achievements. "I'm fully invested in making it work, but I realized the limitations I have as a manager to make it happen," she says. It hasn't been necessary to talk about the consequences if Shauna fails to meet the goal—there are natural consequences in Bliss's high-performing culture. If you don't succeed, you don't get the better assignments.

Amy Gallo is a contributing editor at Harvard Business Review and the author of the *HBR Guide to Managing Conflict at Work*.

Chapter 12
When to Grant a Promotion or Raise

by Amy Gallo

Managers who want to recognize employees for good work have many tools at their disposal. One of the more traditional ways to reward a top performer is to give her a promotion or raise, or both. Even if you don't openly talk about this in your performance review session (as discussed in chapter 8, "Delivering an Effective Performance Review"), it's often something a manager will think about—or an employee will ask about—around formal appraisal time.

But how can you know whether someone is ready for the next challenge or deserving of that bump in pay? Human resource policies and company culture often dictate when and how people move up in a company. However,

Adapted from content posted on hbr.org on January 12, 2011

managers in most companies have a good deal of input into the decision and, in some cases, they are the ultimate decision makers. Whether you have this authority or not, you need to make promotions and raises part of an ongoing discussion with employees about their performance.

What the Experts Say

According to Herminia Ibarra, the Cora Chaired Professor of Leadership and Learning and Faculty Director of the INSEAD Leadership Initiative, "Many times a manager feels responsible for finding their people their next step in the organization." Managers should make these decisions about promotions and raises carefully. "I think who an organization promotes is a very strong index of their core culture," says Susan David, codirector of the Institute of Coaching, founding director of Evidence Based Psychology. Managers should recognize that who they reward sends a signal to the rest of the organization. Therefore, they need to be sure they are endorsing behavior that is in line with the organization's values. For example, an employee who exceeds his targets but treats his team members poorly should not be rewarded in an organization that values teamwork.

Similarly, the way an organization promotes people has implications for an individual's success. Organizations often assume that a promotion should involve giving star performers responsibility for managing more people and developing—rather than just executing—strategy. "Yet these are not areas of genius for all. Many organizations lose some of their best operational people because they create single pathways to organizational success," says David. It's possible to reward people in other ways. "Organizations [that] create multiple, flexible pathways to success will keep their best people, keep them engaged, and keep them for longer," she says. Next time you are trying to decide whether to recognize strong performance with a promotion or raise, follow these principles.

Assess current performance using multiple sources

As a first step, make sure the employee is able to do the job you are considering promoting her into. Take a look at her performance. "There will be markers even in the current job that show how they'll do in the new role," says David. She recommends you use multisource feedback: Draw not only on your own assessment but also on others'. It is especially important to seek input from people who interact with the employees in ways that you don't. Talk to peers, team members, and people she manages. In some cases, you may find that she's already doing parts of the new job. "Some people do their job as it is described and some enlarge their job; they innovate around the parameters of the job. That's the best evidence of all—when they're already doing the job," says Ibarra.

Consider the "competence-challenge balance"

"We all want to be and feel we are good at things. We also have the need to feel we are growing and learning," says David. A good indicator that you may need to promote someone is if he expresses a desire to learn more and take on a new challenge. Your goal-setting discussion will help you assess this. People who are particularly good at their jobs may quickly master them and need to be stretched. "If in their current jobs employees are reaching points where they are overqualified, this is a strong risk factor for disengagement and loss of those employees," says David. You need to constantly assess your people and be sure they are working at the edges of their abilities. If they are performing well but not learning anything new, a promotion or an alternative assignment may be best for both the individual and the organization.

Make sure it's a good match

Before promoting someone into a new role, consider whether it's something she will enjoy doing. Many managers fail to consider that just because someone is good at a job, doesn't mean she will take pleasure in it. "One of the greatest tools a manager can use is an authentic, honest conversation with the individual," explains David. Ask your employee whether she is interested in and excited about the new responsibilities. If not, consider creating an alternative role that stretches her, fulfills her, and fills a need in the organization.

Experiment before making the job permanent

Occasionally, you may need more information to judge the employee's expected performance in a new role. As Ibarra says, "It gets tricky when performance in a current role is not a good predictor of performance in a new role." In these cases, design an assignment that is similar to the tasks and challenges of the new job to test the employee's ability. Be transparent with the employee about this experiment. Make it short-term, and outline clear success criteria and an evaluation timeline. Be careful, though—you don't want to invisibly promote your people without recognizing their contributions. Providing more responsibility without a corresponding change in title or raise can sap motivation.

Determine fair compensation

With some promotions, it may be obvious how much of a raise you should give based on how much others doing the same job are paid. However, many job changes are not as clear cut. The employee may be retaining some of her former responsibilities while taking on new ones. Create a job description for the new role. Take a look at all her duties and try to benchmark them against other jobs in the company or in the broader employment market. If you don't have similar positions in the organization, look at increases that went with other promotions in the organization. If most promotions come with a particular increase in salary, stick with a similar percentage.

Know when to say no

"There are people who will ask for a promotion even if they're not ready," says Ibarra. Your job is to help calibrate those requests. If your employee raises the idea of a promotion but you worry he's not ready, have an open discussion to hear his reasoning and share your concerns. Be clear about what competencies or experiences he needs to gain to be promoted and create an action plan for how he can do that. Provide him with the tasks and assignments he needs to expand his skills.

Because of a limited budget, you may have to say no to someone who is deserving. Or there may not be the right opportunity. To promote, David says, "there needs to be a strategic need in the organization" that this person can meet. These can be tough conversations. Be honest and transparent. Explain the rationale, and be sure the employee understands that you value him. Give him stretch goals that help prepare him for the future when the company is better positioned to give him a promotion or raise.

Consider other ways to motivate

Most important, find other ways to keep the employee engaged. "Leaders are often comforted by their capacity to give a raise or a promotion because these strategies are seen as tangible and executable. However, while these extrinsic motivators are a useful and important part of keeping employees engaged, they are certainly not the only ones," says David. Instead, rely on intrinsic motivators, such as recognizing contributions, providing opportunities to gain new skills or experiences, and supporting autonomy and choice within a job (see chapter 7, "Recognize Good Work in a Meaningful Way"). For example, you may have leeway as a manager to make modifications to the employee's current position so that he is spending half of his time on his current job and the other half on new, more challenging responsibilities. Doing this may be more motivational in the long run and can often inspire loyalty. "Overreliance on pay and promotion as motivators leads to an organizational culture that is very transactional and disengaged," says David. Employees who feel valued are likely to wait out the hard times.

Principles to Remember

Do:

- Make sure your people are working at the edge of their abilities

- Create an assignment that helps you assess whether the employee will excel in a new role

- Find other ways beyond raises and promotions to motivate your people

Don't:

- Say no to a request for a raise or promotion without a clear explanation

- Rely solely on your assessment of the employee's performance without asking others for input

- Assume that a promotion alone will make the employee happy

WHAT PEOPLE ARE SAYING ON HBR.ORG

Employee turnover is thought to be one of the biggest upcoming costs and challenges for companies.

If that's the case, companies need to be proactive in keeping their top players around. Extrinsic motivators like money and promotions are great, but they're not enough to keep people engaged and motivated. In a

(continued)

(continued)

Towers Watson white paper "Turbocharging Employee Engagement: The Power of Recognition from Managers," a main finding is that "strong manager performance in recognizing employee performance increases engagement by almost 60%."

Real-time recognition for tasks well done and employees aligning themselves with company values is a powerful tool not to be overlooked. **Recognition (and rewards) are key to maintaining a motivated workforce.**

—Posted by Sarah

My current position is in a not-for-profit community healthcare facility. Funding is primarily through grants and Medicare or Medicaid. These sources have already been shrinking and more cuts are coming. There have been no bonuses for two years, and raises vanished before that. In addition, more responsibility is a growing burden for staff.

Combine that with the economic hardship of the employees' families and the need for other types of recognition and reward becomes imperative—otherwise, they will be off to find higher-paying jobs.

Your idea of an employee ". . . spending half of his time on his current job and the other half on new, more challenging responsibilities," then, for us, also **has an additional positive effect—more gets done by fewer staff and it helps to prevent burnout by providing variation in tasks, duties, and new coworkers.**

—Posted by Betty

Case Study 1: A New Role for the Firm and the Employee

Elise Giannasi was hired by a strategy consulting firm as the executive assistant to the managing partner. A year into the job, she was receiving glowing reviews and Shanti Nayak, the firm's director of people, says it was clear that she was a star performer. In particular, Shanti noted that Elise had done a great job of building relationships with clients. Her relationships had been instrumental in setting up key appointments and ensuring that bills got paid. The managing partner felt she was ready to move up. But according to Shanti, "there was no typical role for people to move into unless they were on the traditional consultant path."

At the time, the firm didn't have a staff member dedicated solely to business development. People throughout the firm were doing it as an "extracurricular" task. However, the tough economic climate forced the firm to develop a much more formalized process and needed someone to be responsible for it. Shanti explains that they had two debates going on simultaneously: Was this a role they needed? And, if so, was Elise the right person for the role? While Elise was doing small pieces of client development already, she had never filled a role like this before. Shanti knew that Elise had worked hard to develop the right relationships both inside and outside the firm, and she had confidence Elise could do it. When she talked to others in the firm, they endorsed her assessment. In the end, Shanti says, "It felt like a risk worth taking." Shanti explained that since this was a new position, it was difficult to decide how much to pay Elise once she was promoted.

They looked at what other promotions carried in terms of a raise—in particular, the percentage increase that associates received when they became senior associates. Elise was given a similar percentage increase and a new title: manager of business development.

Case Study 2: An Apprenticeship Model for On-the-Job Learning

When Sarah Vania joined the International Rescue Committee as the senior human resource partner, she was particularly impressed with Nicole Clemons, an HR administrator. Nicole was studying for her master's degree while working full time. She commuted two hours by bus to her job, using that time to study. Nicole had always received very good reviews. Sarah thought, "Here's a high-potential person who has earned her right to development." When Sarah sat down with her for their first review together, Nicole asked, "What's the path ahead for me?" She had applied for an open HR partner role, but because it was two steps up from her current role, the organization didn't feel she was ready. Without a logical next step, however, Nicole would be stuck in her current role. "As a manager, I owed her a career path, but I didn't have the budget to create a new role and hire a new admin," says Sarah.

Instead, she decided to create an alternative role for Nicole. Nicole would continue her duties as an HR administrator but also take on two of Sarah's client groups to manage. This apprentice model would allow Nicole to learn on the job what it means to be an HR partner, with Sarah providing her feedback and support. "It helps her learn in a manageable, supported way, rather than trial by fire," explains Sarah. Sarah spoke with the leaders of each client group. She made it clear that although Nicole was still learning the role, she would make their groups her first priority and Sarah would be there if any issues came up. "I asked for their help and explained the benefit," says Sarah. Nicole has since taken on more responsibility, and Sarah says she is well on her way to qualifying for the partner role.

———————

Amy Gallo is a contributing editor at Harvard Business Review and the author of the *HBR Guide to Managing Conflict at Work*.

Chapter 13
Tips for Record Keeping

To prepare for annual reviews, many managers find it useful to keep a file (electronic or hard copy) on every employee's performance and update it throughout the year. Documenting employee performance entails special legal considerations, so consult your human resource manager or internal legal team. If you don't have either resource in your organization, consult a lawyer who specializes in employment law. This is especially advisable when a person's performance is beginning to suffer or if you may need to fire them.

Here are a few things to consider when preparing employee records:

- Record the date and specifics of what occurred: "Jane started sending detailed agendas prior to our weekly meeting with marketing, thereby allowing everyone time to prepare and send adjustments as necessary. This helped the team dive in and cover a large number of topics in a short period of time."

- Stick to the facts: Note the behaviors (for example, Joe's follow-up e-mail campaigns increased sales by 10%) rather than judgments (for example, Mary doesn't know how to manage her time).

- Whenever possible, make your notes on the same day that you've given someone feedback, while it's still fresh in your mind.

- Hang on to e-mails or notes that highlight the accomplishments of your employee, whether they're instances you've noticed yourself or praise from others.

- For performance issues, document the issue and the next steps, including timelines, action items, training, specific goals, and expected outcomes.

- Check in (via e-mail or a face-to-face meeting) with other people who are in a position to evaluate your employee's performance, such as direct reports, clients, vendors, and peers. Ask for feedback on qualities or behaviors, including specific examples that support their observations. Document their feedback, and add it to your file.

- Request regular informal progress reports from your employee that explain how their work is progressing, as well as any concerns or problems they may be having. This will tip you off if there are any issues brewing in your employee's performance and give you the heads-up about what they plan to do next.

When it comes time to conduct your employee's annual review, the bulk of the work will already be done, since you'll have kept such good notes. Your task will then be merely to review and find common themes, rather than rack your brain for highlights or relying on only the most recent performance.

Section 3
Tough Topics

Chapter 14
How to Help an Underperformer

by Amy Gallo

As a manager, you can't accept underperformance. It's frustrating, it's time-consuming, and it can demoralize the other people on your team. But what do you do about an employee whose performance isn't up to snuff? How do you provide them with the feedback they need and help turn around the problematic behavior? And how long do you let it go on before you cut your losses? By facing the issue head-on and creating a correction plan with your employee, you can set your underperformer on the path for improvement.

What the Experts Say

Your company may have a prescribed way of handling an underperformer, but most of those recommended

Adapted from content posted on hbr.org on June 23, 2014

processes aren't that useful, says Jean-François Manzoni, INSEAD professor and coauthor of the book *The Set-Up-to-Fail Syndrome: How Good Managers Cause Great People to Fail.* "When you talk to senior executives, they'll usually acknowledge that those don't work," he says. So it's up to you as the manager to figure out what to do. "When people encounter an issue with underperformance, they really are on their own," says Joseph Weintraub, coauthor of *The Coaching Manager: Developing Top Talent in Business.*

Here's how to stage a productive intervention.

Don't ignore the problem

Too often, underperformance issues go unaddressed. "Most performance problems aren't dealt with directly," says Weintraub. "More often, instead of taking action, the manager will transfer the person somewhere else or let him stay put without doing anything." This is the wrong approach. Never allow underperformance to fester on your team. It's rare that these situations resolve themselves, and they will likely get worse. "You'll become more and more irritated and that's going to show and make the person uncomfortable," says Manzoni. If a problem arises, take steps toward solving it as soon as possible.

Consider what's causing the problem

Is the person a poor fit for the job? Do they lack the necessary skills? Or have they just misunderstood expectations? When it comes to performance, it's common to find mismatches between what managers and employees think is important, Weintraub explains. Consider the role you might be playing in the problem. "You may have contributed to the negative situation," says Manzoni. "After all, it's rare that it's all the subordinate's fault just as it's rare that it's all the boss's." Don't focus exclusively on what the underperformer needs to do to remedy the situation—think about what changes you can make as well.

Ask others what you might be missing

Before you act, look at the problem objectively. Talk to the person's previous boss or someone who's worked with them, or conduct a 360 review. When approaching other people, though, do it carefully and confidentially. Manzoni suggests you say something like: "I'm worried that my frustration may be clouding my judgment. All I can see are the mistakes he's making. I want to make an honest effort to see what I'm missing." Look for evidence that proves your assumptions wrong.

Talk to the underperformer

Once you've checked in with others, talk to the employee directly. Explain exactly what you're observing, point to ways the team's work is affected, and make clear that you want to help. Manzoni suggests the conversation go something like this: "I'm seeing issues with your performance. I believe that you can do better and I know that I may be contributing to the problem. So how do we get out of this? How do we improve?" It's important to engage the person in brainstorming solutions. "Ask them to come up with ideas," says Weintraub. Don't expect an immediate response though. They may need time to digest your feedback and come back later with some proposals.

Confirm that the person is coachable

In most cases, the next step would be to arrange ongoing feedback or coaching sessions. But you can't coach someone who doesn't agree that they need help. In the initial conversation—and throughout the intervention—the employee must acknowledge the problem. "If someone says, 'I am who I am' or implies that they're not going to change, then you've got to make a decision whether you can live with the issue and at what cost," says Weintraub. On the other hand, if you see a willingness to change and a genuine interest in improving, chances are you can work together to turn things around.

Make a plan

Once you've confirmed that the person is coachable, create a concrete plan for what both you and the employee are going to do differently, agreeing on measurable actions so you can mark progress. Write down the specific goals to be met and plan the execution of these tasks by assigning start and end dates. Then identify what resources the employee needs to accomplish those goals, whether time, equipment, or assistance or coaching from others. Once you've outlined everything on paper, ask them how they feel about the plan, answering any questions or clarifying any points as necessary. You don't want them to make promises they can't meet, and you want to make sure you're in agreement moving forward. Then, give them time. "Everyone needs time to change and maybe learn or acquire new skills," says Weintraub.

Regularly monitor progress

Once the conversation is over, the manager's work isn't done. You must follow up to make sure that the correction plan is being implemented. Ask the person to check in with you regularly, or set up specific dates in the future to check progress. It may be helpful to ask the employee if they have someone they'd like you to enlist in the effort. Weintraub suggests you ask: "Is there anyone you trust who can provide me with feedback about how well you're doing in making these changes?" Doing this sends a positive message: "It says I want this to work and I want you to feel comfortable; I'm not going to sneak around your back."

Respect confidentiality

Along the way, it's important to keep what's happening confidential—while also letting others know you're working on the underperformance problem. Manzoni admits that this is a tricky balancing act. Don't discuss the specific details with others, he says. But you might tell them something like: "Bill and I are working together on his output and lately we've had good discussions. I need your help in being as positive and supportive as you can."

Praise and reward positive change

If the person makes positive changes, say so. Make clear that you've noticed developments, and reward your employee accordingly. "At some point, if the nonper-former has improved, be sure to take them off the death spiral. You want a team that can make mistakes and learn from them," says Weintraub.

If there isn't improvement, take action

Of course, if things don't get better, change the tenor of the discussion. "At some point you leave coaching and get into the consequences speech. You might say, 'Let me be very clear that this is the third time this has hap-pened, and since your behavior hasn't changed, I need to explain the consequences,'" says Weintraub. Disciplin-ary actions, particularly letting someone go, shouldn't be taken lightly. "When you fire somebody, it not only affects that person, but also you, the firm, and everybody around you," says Manzoni.

While it may be painful to fire someone, it may be the best option for your team. "It's disheartening if you see the person next to you not performing," says Weintraub. Manzoni elaborates: "The person you're asking to leave is only one of the stakeholders. The people left behind are the more important ones . . . When people feel the pro-cess is fair, they're willing to accept a negative outcome."

Principles to Remember

Do:

- Take action as soon as possible—the sooner you intervene the better

- Consider how you might be contributing to the performance issues

- Make a concrete, measurable plan for improvement

Don't:

- Assume the issue is resolved after one conversation

- Try to coach someone who is unwilling to admit that there's an issue

- Talk about specific performance issues with others on the team

Case Study 1: Commit to the Time Investment

Allie Rogovin managed a five-person team at Teach For America when she brought in Max (name has been changed) as a recruiting coordinator. The job had two main responsibilities: completing administrative duties that supported the recruiting team and managing special projects. Allie recognized that the administrative component wasn't that exciting, so she "let him know that the better and faster he completed these tasks, the more time he'd have for the fun projects." But before long, Max was struggling with the core part of his role. "I realized a couple months into the job he wasn't getting his administrative duties done in time," she admits.

Allie started by giving Max an action plan template. She asked him to take 20 minutes at the end of each day to enter and prioritize all of his tasks. She then reviewed his list every evening and gave him input on how he might shuffle his priorities for the next day. They also

WHAT PEOPLE ARE SAYING ON HBR.ORG

Yes, it's important to gauge whether the employee is coachable. It is equally important to **determine if the manager is competent to coach the employee through the process.** Too many managers lack the skill or patience to help the employee work their way through the performance issue. The best manager-teacher-coach will be flexible in helping the employee utilize skills and talents different from the manager's rather than using the old, stale, "Here, let me show you how it's done."
—Posted by Mike

Do you have the right person in the right position? And if so, have you translated the organization's vision to their position? **Too many times we put people in positions, thinking they are the right person, and then we don't help them succeed.** We don't translate the vision of the company into their specific area and set specific key performance indicators for that person or team.

So, when you address this problem, remember to go back to the basic, foundational reason for that person's position, and let them know how it helps achieve the overall vision.
—Posted by RJ

started meeting three times a week instead of just once a week.

"He was a very valuable team member, and I knew he could do a good job. That made me want to invest time in working with him," she says. She continued meeting with Max regularly and reviewing his priorities for three months: "I didn't think it was going to be that long but I wanted to see that he was building new habits." Max still occasionally missed deadlines but he was showing definite signs of improvement.

"We tweaked the plan along the way and he eventually got into the swing of things," she says. "I frankly wouldn't have done it if I didn't see huge potential in him."

Case Study 2: Recognize When Change Won't Happen

Bill Wright (not his real name), a business developer at a residential building company, hired a new project manager last summer. We'll call him Jack. Right from the start, Bill saw performance issues. One of Jack's primary responsibilities was to develop small projects. That meant defining the scope of the project, talking with homeowners, negotiating with subcontractors, and coordinating with design professionals. "He was taking too long to get things done. What should have taken days, was taking three to four weeks," Bill says. This was problematic for many reasons: "I was supposed to be billing his time to the client but I couldn't bill for the amount of time he was putting in. Plus, I had disgruntled homeowners who were wondering why things were taking so long."

Bill met with Jack weekly to review the current workload, prioritize tasks, and resolve any issues. "I wanted to help him move things forward, but eventually I got so frustrated that I started to take projects over," Bill says. At Jack's 90-day review, Bill had a frank conversation with his employee about the consequences of not being able to turn around his performance. "When I asked what he needed, Jack said that he wanted more than an hour of my time each week to get more input on his work. I said I was happy to do that and asked him to go ahead and schedule a regular meeting time," Bill says. But Jack never followed up or put any additional time on Bill's calendar.

"It was very clear that it wasn't working out. There were never signs of any progress." That's when Bill sat Jack down and made it clear that his job was on the line. Again, there was no change in behavior, so several weeks later, he let Jack go. "I look back on it and realize I made a bad hire. I recently hired his replacement and it's like night and day. He already gets the job."

————————

Amy Gallo is a contributing editor at Harvard Business Review and the author of the *HBR Guide to Managing Conflict at Work.*

Chapter 15
Delivering Criticism to a Defensive Employee

by Holly Weeks

How do you handle giving unfavorable feedback to someone who will surely take it badly—and I mean *really*
badly? Think shouting, tears, defensiveness, accusations,
personal attacks, revising history, twisting words—pick
your nightmare.

Consider the case of Melissa, who was the team leader
on a recently concluded project that had been an unsat-
isfactory experience for the whole group. For most of the
team, the project was a disappointment from the start:

Adapted from content posted on hbr.org on August 12, 2015

team members were assigned, not self-selected; it was not a high-profile project; and the deliverables were really important only for Melissa's mentor's research. Melissa's role was not a powerful one. She was first among equals and the liaison to management, but had more responsibility than actual authority. The carrot that management held out to members of the team was that this was a stepping-stone project: if the results were satisfactory, they could anticipate higher-profile projects going forward.

James, a team member working from a remote location, handled the situation by making the project a lower priority than his other work. He often finished his tasks late or failed to deliver at all, but he knew Melissa would pick up the slack because it was in her mentor's interest for someone to do so. He considered this a pragmatic solution—he had a lot of work to do. His miscalculation, however, was to assume that the team's work would be seen only as a whole. Instead, when the project ended, Melissa was asked to recommend individuals from the team for a new, more important project. James would not be one of them, and Melissa had scheduled a feedback session with him to let him know.

Melissa knew the conversation would not go well. James was known to shout at people, distort their words, accuse them of victimizing him, and more. Melissa's own temperament was unlike his, and the thought of giving James negative feedback was a nightmare.

How should Melissa handle the situation?

When we fear someone's reaction, most of us look for techniques to make the other person act differently.

But when they get disagreeable feedback, people generally repeat tactics that they've had success with in the past—that's why they use them. In the face of negative feedback, it's likely that James will be surprised and angry. He's likely to believe that Melissa misrepresented the project's outcome and is scapegoating him, robbing him of the only benefit of four months' work. In James' view, how he responds makes sense: Melissa is not reliable, not his boss, and intends to hurt him. Why would he act differently? He wants her to back off.

Melissa foresees that scenario, but her temperament makes her vulnerable to choosing what business theorist Chris Argyris calls "defensive strategies"—ambiguous, counterproductive behavior chosen to avoid interpersonal discomfort. Examples of this might be Melissa deferring to James, apologizing and agreeing that he is being misused, while stressing that she is just the messenger. Or she might e-mail the message, letting him simmer in solitude. Or she could ask someone else to tell him. Any of these would protect Melissa from immediate discomfort, but they also signal weak competence.

Defensive strategies become "skilled incompetence," Argyris says—we get really good at avoiding the difficult bits, but can't reach good outcomes and never really accomplish our goals. That can't be recommended as a feedback approach, even if it seems better than butting heads.

Yet if Melissa does try to toughen up and match James' confrontational style, even though she knows firsthand that won't be well received, it's sure to backfire. Emotions will rise, and the conversation will degenerate on both sides, destroying the relationship and potentially both of their reputations.

Melissa needs to try a different approach. One tactic is to focus on immunizing herself against her own vulnerability to James' difficult behavior. This is like a scientist who, when studying how a pathogen compromises a cell, focuses on the cell, not the bug.

How would Melissa self-immunize against James' outbursts? By recognizing that *she* has to react to the tactic for it to work. Instead of reacting, she can neutralize how she responds, without giving in or giving up what she has to say. To get there, she can use a blueprint that pulls together three attributes of speaking well in tough moments: clear content, neutral tone, and temperate phrasing.

> **Clear content:** Let your words do your work for you. Say what you mean. Imagine that you are a newscaster and that it's important that people understand the information. If your counterpart distorts what you say, repeat it just as you said it the first time.

> **Neutral tone:** Tone is the nonverbal part of the message you're delivering. It's the inflection in your voice, your facial expressions, and your conscious and unconscious body language. These all carry emotional weight in a difficult conversation. It's hard to use a neutral tone when your emotions are running high. That's why you need to practice it ahead of time, so you become accustomed to using it. Think of the

classic neutrality of NASA communications in tough situations: "Houston, we have a problem."

Temperate phrasing: There are lots of different ways to say what you have to say. Some are considered and nonconfrontational; some baldly provoke your counterpart with loaded language. If your counterpart dismisses, resists, or throws back your words, he's not likely to hold on to your content—so choose your words carefully. (See the sidebar "Phrases to Make Sure You're Heard.")

PHRASES TO MAKE SURE YOU'RE HEARD

By Amy Gallo

- "My perspective is based on the following assumptions . . ."

- "I came to this conclusion because . . ."

- "I'd love to hear your reaction to what I just said."

- "Do you see any flaws in my reasoning?"

- "Do you see the situation differently?"

Adapted from the *HBR Guide to Managing Conflict at Work* (product #15006), Harvard Business Review Press, 2015.

Amy Gallo is a contributing editor at Harvard Business Review and the author of the *HBR Guide to Managing Conflict at Work*.

Clear content, neutral tone, and temperate phrasing are a package deal. Melissa won't get good results if she uses temperate phrasing, but mixes her message with a lot of contradictory body language. Nor will it work well if she softens her content because she thinks it is too blunt. Being blunt is a characteristic of intemperate phrasing, not of content. So softening the content to fix a problem of phrasing won't get her where she wants to go.

If Melissa says to James, "In February, March, and April, the team didn't get the deliverables you committed to on the dates you agreed to," her content is clear and her phrasing is temperate. We have to imagine that her tone is neutral, but Melissa can do it. If she says, "With those omissions, I can't stand behind a recommendation for you," she is clear and temperate again. We do understand that the news is not good and James is still likely to dip into his arsenal of difficult tactics. But Melissa is on solid ground, neither altering her message nor responding to his tactics. With this blueprint in place, repetition can be a good friend: if James challenges her or distorts her message, Melissa can repeat what she has said, rather than following James down a rabbit hole. When it's time to end the meeting, she can say something simple such as: "Thank you for meeting with me. [Short pause.] I wish this had worked out differently."

Will James be happy with this conversation? I think not. Nobody likes unfavorable feedback. But remember, when delivering negative feedback to someone who's likely to get defensive, it's not your job to make the other person feel better. It's your job to convey the information in a clear, neutral, and temperate way—by sticking to the facts and to the blueprint.

———————

Holly Weeks publishes, teaches, and consults on communications issues. She is Adjunct Lecturer in Public Policy at the Harvard Kennedy School and the author of *Failure to Communicate: How Conversations Go Wrong and What You Can Do to Right Them* (Harvard Business School Press, 2008).

Chapter 16
How to Give Star Performers Productive Feedback

by Amy Gallo

As counterintuitive as it may seem, giving feedback to a top performer can be even tougher than giving it to an underperformer or a combative employee. Top performers may not have obvious development needs, and in identifying those needs, you can feel like you're being nitpicky or overdemanding. In addition, top performers may not be used to hearing constructive feedback and may bristle at the slightest hint that they're not perfect.

But giving your stars good feedback is essential to keeping them engaged, focused, and motivated. Luckily,

Adapted from content posted on hbr.org on December 3, 2009

feedback discussions do not need to be unpleasant, especially with top performers. Instead of dreading your next conversation with them, think of it as an exciting opportunity to celebrate success and discuss what's next.

What the Experts Say

Don't be tempted to bend the rules for top performers. No matter who the receiver is, follow good feedback practice. Do your homework: Gather data and details to support your point of view. Always describe behaviors, not traits. Don't dwell on the past; focus on what the employee can change in the future. Check for understanding and clarify and agree on the next steps and a fair way to measure progress.

That said, feedback for your top performers does require special care. Don't assume your star is perfect. INSEAD professor Jean-François Manzoni says, "Everyone has some room for improvement, in this job or the next, within our current set of capabilities or a broader set that will likely come in handy in the future." You do your stars a disservice if you fail to help them figure out how they can continue to grow.

When conducting your research, remember that results don't always speak for themselves. High performers often have great results, yet it's important to understand *how* they achieve those results and at what cost. Unfortunately, they often get results by forgoing other things, such as caring for their people, building alliances with others, or maintaining a healthy work-life balance. In addition, top performers' strengths may often be their weaknesses. For instance, an employee who has the ability to stay out of workplace drama and focus on her work may be perceived by peers as unapproachable. Think carefully about the behaviors that have enabled your star to succeed—they may be the same behaviors holding her back.

To make the most of your feedback sessions, regularly discuss these three topics: current performance, the next performance frontier, and future goals and aspirations.

Express gratitude for current performance

Many managers make the mistake of assuming that their top performers already know how well they are doing. Always start your feedback session by specifically stating what your star has accomplished. Show gratitude for their contributions and successes. As Manzoni says, "Advice is more likely to be welcome if it builds on comments acknowledging and celebrating this year's performance and is clearly positioned at helping the subordinate continue to develop beyond the current role and capability set." Constructive feedback is more easily received if it is preceded by genuine appreciation for hard work. Given how valuable your star is to you and your organization, you can't express enough how much you value them.

WHAT PEOPLE ARE SAYING ON HBR.ORG

If you're not getting constructive feedback from your manager, you don't need to wait for review time to ask. Explain to your manager that you want feedback. After a project milestone or a particularly important meeting, ask your manager if she has any feedback for you.

(continued)

(continued)

You can ask questions such as, "Do you think I handled that OK?" or "Do you have any advice about how I might do better next time?" Be prepared to ask follow-up questions, especially if you are a star performer. Chances are you're doing great and your manager will need to be prompted to think about how you can improve. Many managers are inexperienced in giving feedback, and the more you can be clear about what you are looking for, the more helpful it will be to [your manager].

—Posted by Amy

I've seen star performers leave organizations because they are starved for constructive feedback from their managers. **They often assume that their manager doesn't care about their performance because of the lack of feedback they receive.**

—Posted by Gabrielle

What I find useful is to **give feedback that helps shape the person's personal goals as well as professional goals.** For example, I have one employee who is passionate about the Middle East and Arabic studies. So we found a way at UniversalGiving to let her find and

source NGOs (nongovernmental organizations) in that area. It fits her goals, and it fits ours. She moved from Executive Assistance (which she did very well) to NGO Marketing.
—Posted by Pamela

Research is clear on the importance of feedback—both positive and negative—on employee engagement. It's those employees who are ignored who just don't care to give their all. Gallup proved this in a study showing:

- Managers who focus on employee strengths have 61% engaged employees and 1% actively disengaged.

- Managers who focus on employee weaknesses have 45% engaged employees and 22% actively disengaged.

- Managers who ignore their employees have 2% engaged employees and 40% actively disengaged.

It's critical to note that it is the direct manager's behavior that has the most impact on engagement. Too many, however, prefer to just close the door and ignore their teams.
—Posted by Derek

Discuss obstacles to their development

Your top performer is likely committed to self-improvement—that's probably one of the ways he became a top performer. As a manager, it's your responsibility to help him determine how to keep improving. Tap into that commitment and engage your high performer in a discussion about how he might achieve the next level of performance, whether it is a new sales target or a promotion. Discussions should include acknowledging what might be standing in the way and how he can overcome those obstacles. These don't need to be negative conversations, however. Manzoni had a particularly good manager who adeptly helped him think about what was next and how he could get there. As Manzoni says, "I never felt criticized. Instead, I walked into his office six feet tall, and I came out of it nine feet tall."

Identify future goals and aspirations

Once you and your star have agreed on where she is headed, ask about her motivation and values. Ask prompting questions such as "What do you want to be known for?" or "What matters most to you?" This will give her a chance to reflect on her career path and how this current role and the next performance frontier fit in. It will give your high performer what Jamie Harris, a senior consultant at Interaction Associates, describes as a "window into greater awareness about what enables [your star] to succeed in the current situation and what she wants to achieve next." It will also allow you to figure out how you can align the person's motivations with those of the company. Harris says, "Some people perform well in any context, but people will almost always perform well when their own excellence is aligned with that of the organization."

As you give feedback to high performers, solicit their input on how you are doing as a manager. Ask questions such as "How can I continue to support your high performance?" or "What can we do as an organization to keep getting better and supporting your great work?" This is important because, as Harris says, it "shows that you're their ally in achieving what they want to achieve. This also helps cement their connection to the organization."

Frequency is key

In giving feedback to your stars, frequency is crucial. Harris warns that you shouldn't be tempted to leave your high performers alone. He says, "The higher the performer, the more frequently you should be providing feedback." Don't wait for review time. You and your company depend on retaining top performers. Therefore, it is a wise investment of your time and energy to support and develop them.

Principles to Remember

Do:

- Give both positive and constructive feedback to high performers regularly

- Identify development areas, even if there are only a few

- Focus on the future and ask about motivations and goals

Don't:

- Presume your stars have reached the limits of their performance

- Leave your top performers alone

- Assume your best workers know how appreciated they are

Case Study: Reframing Feedback in the Context of Long-Term Goals

Gretchen Anderson has worked with many young, ambitious professionals throughout her career. During her tenure at a strategy consulting firm, Gretchen managed a particularly ambitious consultant named Melissa. Melissa was an extremely hardworking associate—so hardworking that Gretchen and others at the firm were concerned she would not be able to sustain her accelerated pace. Her reviews consisted mostly of positive feedback about her performance. However, Gretchen felt she needed to address the pace of Melissa's work: "I didn't want her to be another burnout story."

Upon hearing the feedback, Melissa became very emotional. She didn't understand why Gretchen would thank her for her hard work and then tell her to stop working so hard. She felt she should be the judge of when she was working too much. In each of Melissa's feedback sessions, this issue became a source of intense emotion for Melissa and conflict with Gretchen. Melissa regularly asked for follow-up sessions to keep discussing the issue and grilling Gretchen about the fairness of the feedback.

After a half-dozen conversations, Gretchen decided she needed to find a way to reframe the issue so Melissa could understand what was at stake. Instead of starting the sessions focused on current performance, Gretchen began by asking Melissa about her long-term career goals. Gretchen said, "I knew I couldn't change her nature, but I could focus on helping her change her behavior as long as I could get her in the right frame of mind first."

Melissa said she wanted to be promoted to manager as soon as possible. With that goal as the backdrop, Gretchen was able to explain more clearly to Melissa the consequences of her work pace: As a manager, Melissa would need to set an example for her associates. Also, if she was constantly working at capacity, how would she handle a last-minute client request? Melissa needed to figure out how to build more spaces into her schedule so that when she became a manager, she'd be able to serve her clients well and treat her associates fairly. Melissa's drive to work hard was not going to go away, so instead of battling that, Gretchen gave her a reason she could relate to for modifying her behavior.

———————

Amy Gallo is a contributing editor at Harvard Business Review and the author of the *HBR Guide to Managing Conflict at Work*.

Chapter 17
Prioritizing Feedback— Even When Time Is Short

by Daisy Wademan Dowling

Virtually all of the young executives I work with want to be good managers and mentors. They just don't have the time—or so they believe. "I could either bring in a new deal or I could take one of my people out for lunch to talk about their career," a financial services leader told me recently. "In this industry and in this market, which one do you think I'm going to pick?"

Good question. It's not easy to help your employees develop while you're trying to take advantage of every

---

Adapted from the *HBR Guide to Coaching Employees* (product #13990), Harvard Business Review Press, 2015 business opportunity, but you can make it easier on yourself, in part by giving feedback efficiently.

Once you've identified that you need to give feedback to a direct report, make that process more efficient in three ways.

Create a Standard Way In

For the majority of managers, providing feedback—particularly constructive feedback—is stressful and requires significant forethought. How should you bring up the bungled analysis, the hurdles to promotion, or even the meeting that went unusually well? Like chess masters, we spend most of our time contemplating the first move. That's why the key to reducing the time you spend mulling over and preparing for each conversation is to have a standard way in: a simple, routinized way to open discussions about performance.

Keep it simple, and announce directly what's to come. A straightforward "I'm going to give you some feedback" or "Are you open to my coaching on this?" gets immediate attention and sets the right tone. It will make it easier to prepare for the game if you have your opener ready. Furthermore, your direct reports will become familiar with your opener, and that will help them be attuned to and hear the feedback more clearly.

Be Blunt

The number-one mistake executives make in coaching and delivering feedback to their people is being insufficiently candid—typically, because they don't want to be mean. If you've ever used the phrase "Maybe you could..."

in a coaching conversation or asked one of your people to "think about" a performance issue, there's a 99% probability you're not being blunt enough. But the more candid you are, the more likely your direct report is to hear your message, and thus the more likely you are to have impact, and quickly. The trick to being candid without feeling like an ogre? Be honest, be sincere, be personal—while addressing the issue head-on.

The best feedback I ever received came a few years into my career, directly after a terrible meeting I had with senior management in which I had been both unprepared and defensive. As we rode down in the elevator afterward, my boss said quietly, "Next time, I expect you to do better." Don't dance around the issues, and don't let the recipient do so either.

Ask for Playback

If your feedback doesn't stick, you'll need to deliver it a second time—and a third, and a fourth—all of which takes your valuable time and managerial energy. To avoid the need for encore performances, make sure you've made an impact on the first go-round by asking the person to paraphrase what he heard. If he can clearly explain to you—in his own words—what he needs to change or do next, that goes a long way to ensuring he's gotten the message. Then you'll know that the conversation is over and you can get back to other things. If the message is muddled, you can correct it immediately. In either case, you've curtailed the need for future follow-up.

By doing these things regularly (perhaps even daily), you'll not only save yourself and your direct report time, but your employees will feel that you're not just their boss, but a coach. They'll sharpen their skills *and* stay motivated. And for any manager, that's time well spent.

———————

Daisy Wademan Dowling serves as managing director and head of talent development for the Blackstone Group, the global asset management firm. She is also the author of *Remember Who You Are* (Harvard Business School Press, 2004) and a regular contributor to HBR.

Chapter 18

Navigating the Choppy Waters of Cross-Cultural Feedback

by Andy Molinsky

Although many of us don't like to do it, we know that critiquing others' work—ideally in a constructive, polite, empowering manner—is an essential part of our jobs. But does critical feedback work similarly across cultures? Do people in Shanghai provide critical feedback in the same way as people in Stuttgart, Strasbourg, and Stockholm?

Nein, non, and *nej.*

Instead, they confront situations where they do have to adjust their feedback style, and sometimes that's easier

Adapted from content posted on hbr.org on February 15, 2013

said than done. Take the case of Jens, a German executive who was sent by the German corporate headquarters
of his company to improve efficiency at the company's
manufacturing plant in Shanghai. All his efforts, however, seemed to be producing the exact opposite result.
Employee productivity and effectiveness were both going down, and Jens could not figure out what was going
wrong. He was using everything he knew that worked in
Germany—especially in terms of performance feedback.
In fact, he made doubly sure to be just as demanding and
exacting with his Chinese employees as he would have
been with German staff. If his Chinese employees failed
to produce what he was looking for, Jens would be "on it,"
providing immediate critique to get the process moving
back in the right direction. But this approach failed mis-
erably. Rather than improving efficiency, Jens seemed
to be reducing it, and his own bosses from corporate
started to make calls. The entire situation was becoming
a disaster.

It turns out that what worked in Germany in terms of
tough, critical, to-the-point negative feedback was actually demotivating to Jens's new Chinese employees, who
were used to a far gentler feedback style. In Germany, you
typically don't single out specific accomplishments or offer praise unless the accomplishment is truly extraordi-
nary. Employees are expected to do a particular job, and
when they do that job, they do not need to be recognized.
In China—at least at this particular plant—the culture
was quite different. Employees expected more positive
reinforcement rather than pure critique. Positive comments were what motivated them to increase productivity and put forth that extra, discretionary effort.

It took quite some time and effort on Jens's part to recognize this difference and to be willing to adapt his behavior to accommodate the Chinese approach because to him, this motivational style felt awkward and unnatural. He didn't feel like himself when he was "soft" with his employees, and he had serious doubts about the effectiveness of doing so. However, over time and through quite a bit of trial and error, Jens was able to develop a new feedback style that worked in the Chinese setting and also felt acceptable (or acceptable enough) to his German mind-set. It took time and effort, but in the end was quite effective.

Clearly, performance feedback can be very different across cultures, whether you're in Germany, China, the UK, or the US. Given that fact and our interest in becoming effective global managers, what can you do to ensure your style fits the new setting?

- **Learn the new cultural rules.** Many managers I speak with tell me how they had just assumed their style was universal, and that lack of awareness was what initially got them into trouble. How direct and to-the-point are you expected to be? How important is it to save face or protect the social standing of others when delivering feedback in group settings? Learning the cultural code by reading up on the culture and observing it in action is the very first step toward developing cultural fluency.

- **Find a cultural mentor.** In Jens's case, he had a Chinese-born cultural mentor to help guide him out of this quagmire. Although this particular consultant didn't share Jens's German culture, he was globally savvy, having worked in high-level positions in multinational companies for many years. A mentor who appreciates your position as well as the expectations of the new culture can help you craft a new style that fits where you are and that feels authentic to you.

- **Customize your behavior.** Don't assume you have to follow the other culture's behavior to the letter to be successful. You often can create a blend or a hybrid that feels comfortable (enough) for you that is effective in the new setting. Jens, for example, was able to adjust his feedback style to be somewhat less frank than his German approach, and it worked.

As organizations become more global, most of us will be face to face with colleagues of different cultural backgrounds, whether it's abroad or in our own offices. Learning how to navigate difficult conversations and to provide critique across cultures is certainly a challenge. But with these tips in mind, you can face this challenge head-on, no matter what part of the world you're in.

––––––––––––

Andy Molinsky is a professor of International Management and Organizational Behavior at the Brandeis International Business School. He is the author of the book *Global Dexterity: How to Adapt Your Behavior across Cultures without Losing Yourself in the Process* (Harvard Business Review Press, 2013).

Chapter 19
How to Discuss Performance with Your Team

by Rebecca Knight

The majority of this book has been geared toward giving individuals feedback. But you're not always dealing with one person at a time. What if you're assessing a team's work? What type of constructive criticism is appropriate in a group setting? How much is too much? And how should your colleagues help?

Just because you're facing a group of employees, rather than just one, doesn't mean you must hold your tongue. There are a few ways that you can provide feedback to the entire team so that they all benefit.

Adapted from content posted on hbr.org on June 16, 2014

What the Experts Say

Providing feedback isn't solely the team leader's responsibility, according to Mary Shapiro, author of the *HBR Guide to Leading Teams*. For starters, that would be impractical. "You can't be the only one holding everyone accountable because you can't possibly observe everything that's going on," she says. Second, if you're the only one praising or critiquing, group dynamics suffer. "You want to give everyone the opportunity to say his piece," she says. Your job as manager is to ensure that team members are "providing regular constructive feedback," says Roger Schwarz, organizational psychologist and author of *Smart Leaders, Smarter Teams*. "There needs to be an expectation within the team that this is a shared leadership responsibility," he says. Here are some principles to help you lay the groundwork for ensuring and enhancing this effective team practice.

Set expectations early

"When a team works well together, it's because its members are operating from the same mind-set and are clear about their goals and their norms," says Schwarz. At the start of a new project, help your direct reports "decide how they're going to work together"—and importantly, how they will "hold each other accountable," says Shapiro. She recommends coming up with an "explicit agreement" about how the team will handle issues like the division of labor and deadlines. Stipulate, for example, that if a colleague knows he is going to miss an important deadline for his portion of a project, he must e-mail the team at least 24 hours in advance. "If someone doesn't follow through on the expectations the team created, he'll get feedback from the group about what happened because he fell short."

Create opportunities for regular check-ins

There's no hard-and-fast rule about how often your team should meet to review how things are going, but in general, "it's better to start out with more structure and relax it over time, than to start out with too little structure and have to impose it later," Shapiro says. When you're in the early stages of creating a project plan, schedule regular check-ins as part of the timeline. "If the team is running smoothly, you can always cancel the meeting."

Ask general questions

Giving and receiving feedback is a skill—and most people are not naturally good at it, says Shapiro. "One of your goals is to develop your team's capacity to give feedback and help people get used to articulating how they feel the team is doing." Take baby steps. At the second or third check-in, ask the group general questions such as, "On a scale of 1 to 5, how well is the team sharing the workload? What needs to change?" As the leader, you're the moderator of this conversation. Once team members have spoken, offer your view about "where the team excels and where it faces challenges," Schwarz adds.

Work your way up to structured reviews

As your team gets accustomed to working together and sharing feedback, "you need to do a deeper dive into how team members are doing at the individual level," says Shapiro. Ask each person to prepare specific reviews of colleagues to be read aloud at the next meeting. "Every team member should say one thing they appreciate about the other members and one thing that would be helpful if they did differently." The aim is to help "people understand how their behavior is impacting others," she says. "If they hear the same kind of feedback from multiple people, that is powerful." When it's your turn, Schwarz recommends validating your observations with others. "Ask: 'Are you seeing things the same way?' Get other people's reactions."

Keep performance issues out in the open

The management mantra for giving individuals feedback is: "Praise in public, criticize in private." But in team settings, this goes out the window, according to Schwarz. "In the traditional view, it's inappropriate to raise issues in a meeting that would make people uncomfortable or put people on the spot." But your job as a leader is not always to make people feel comfortable. When teams have problems, "it should all be out in the open," he says. "You alone can't help people improve; there needs to be a group plan." After you've "harnessed the power of the group" to prompt change, one-on-one conversations with struggling colleagues are then in order, says Shapiro. "Say to them: 'What did you hear from the team? How are you going to do things differently? And how can I help?'"

Foster team relationships

Conflicts between coworkers are inevitable. But, Schwarz says, "you can't just say, 'I'll handle it,' because [as the manager] you can't solve a problem to which you're not a primary stakeholder. You can coach people on how to have difficult conversations, and you can help facilitate those conversations, but team members need to address issues where the interdependencies lie." Help colleagues build trust before problems arise by encouraging open conversation. And, when there is conflict, make sure they understand, they need to "give feedback directly to each other," says Schwarz. Adds Shapiro: "The only way good work gets done is through good relationships—the better the relationship, the better the work."

Debrief every project

At the end of a project or when your team is disbanding, schedule a final check-in to discuss "what worked and what didn't, what should we bring forward and what should we do differently next time," says Schwarz. Take careful notes: the information gleaned in this session should not only be part of the organization's final project review, but also part of each team member's annual performance appraisal, says Shapiro. The objective is to "provide closure on the team and also determine what each member needs to do to further develop," she says.

Principles to Remember

Do:

- Make sure your team understands that feedback is a shared leadership responsibility

- Schedule routine check-in meetings

- Keep the tone positive by encouraging team members to say what they appreciate about others' contributions

Don't:

- Shy away from performance issues

- Deliver your own feedback to the team without asking them how they think they're doing first

- Put yourself in the middle of personality conflicts

Case Study 1: Create Opportunities for Team and Individual Reflection

Once every quarter, Laree Daniel—chief administrative officer of Aflac, the insurance company—assembles an ad hoc team around a particular customer incident for an in-depth feedback session. "I take a customer case study in which we either did very well or very poorly, and I gather everyone that touched the customer in some form," she says.

First, Laree makes sure everyone is up to speed. Team members are given an information packet that includes a write-up of the incident, transcripts of phone calls, copies of customer letters, and copies of the company's responses. Next, she poses a series of questions to the team: What worked well? Where were the gaps? What can we do better?

The goal, she says, is to get the team to reflect on the company's behavior from both the customer's perspective and shareholder's. "This isn't about blame, and I'm not scolding anyone," she says. "I am the facilitator and I make it a neutral environment."

During these feedback meetings, colleagues often have epiphanies. "They realize: 'I didn't know [my behavior] would have that impact,'" she says. "It becomes a dynamic learning experience."

The feedback and information she picks up from those meetings are used to make process improvements. "Often the best ideas come from those people who were closest to the work."

Case Study 2: Focus on Empowering Your Team

David S. Rose, the angel investor and CEO of Gust—a platform for the sourcing and management of early-stage investments—has a simple approach when it comes to giving group feedback. "The goal is not to depress the team," he says. "I try to keep everything upbeat and lay out our strengths and our challenges.

A few years ago, for instance, he was involved in leading a 15-person technical team at a software company. The group's biggest issue was its disappointing B2B product suite. "Customers were unhappy and the front-end salespeople were being yelled at," he says. "As a team, we had some good individual contributors but we needed to get better at working together. I couldn't just walk in and give feedback along the lines of: 'These products are terrible; you're all fired.' We needed to identify the organizational problems and come up with a prescription for a path forward."

He broke the team into subgroups of two or three people, and he tasked each with brainstorming how to manage a particular inter-team challenge. The subgroups then provided feedback to everyone else; based on that, the team developed a strategy to improve workflow and communication. "We came up with a plan and the whole team felt empowered," he says. "We knew what the problems were and we figured out how to solve them."

Within nine months, he says, the products were in far better shape.

———————

Rebecca Knight is a freelance journalist in Boston and a lecturer at Wesleyan University. Her work has been published in the *New York Times, USA Today,* and the *Financial Times.*

Index

Index

Notes

Notes

Notes

Notes

Notes

Notes

Notes

Notes

Notes